EVERYDAY
KETO
BAKING

EVERYDAY KETO BAKING

HEALTHY LOW-CARB RECIPES FOR EVERY OCCASION **ERICA KERWIEN**

FAIR WINDS

Brimming with creative inspiration, how-to projects, and useful information to enrich your everyday life, Quarto Knows is a favorite destination for those pursuing their interests and passions. Visit our site and dig deeper with our books into your area of interest: Quarto Creates, Quarto Cooks, Quarto Homes, Quarto Lives, Quarto Drives, Quarto Explores, Quarto Gifts, or Quarto Kids.

The information in this book is for educational purposes only. It is not intended to replace the advice of a physician or medical practitioner. Please see your health-care provider before beginning any new health program.

TO *COMFY BELLY* READERS
AND RECIPE TESTERS, WHO ARE MY
COOKING FAMILY AND FRIENDS
AND WHO INSPIRE ME TO WRITE
TASTY RECIPES

CONTENTS

CHAPTER 1

GETTING STARTED WITH KETO BAKING

The ketogenic (keto) diet is used for a variety of reasons, from managing diabetes to weight loss, and it's proved very effective. I'll dive into a short explanation of the diet below, but remember that it's always a good idea to consult with a health professional for support, especially if you're considering the keto diet for health reasons.

Your body typically burns fuel in the form of glucose from carbohydrates—mostly because it's more accessible. When food or carbohydrates are not readily available, your liver begins to convert fat, rather than carbs, into fuel. This state of burning fats is called ketosis.

By eating a diet low in carbohydrates and high in fat, you create an environment in your body that favors burning fat. What it takes to get and stay in ketosis varies for each person, and it depends on your age, body weight, gender, and activity level.

To better determine what your goal is for maintaining ketosis, measure the amount of fat to protein to carbohydrates you eat on a daily basis. Here is the general ratio guideline for daily consumption of each type of macronutrient while on the keto diet:

- Fat: 60 to 75 percent of your calories
- Protein: 15 to 30 percent of your calories
- Carbs: 5 to 10 percent of your calories

Note that this can vary by person, depending on how each individual body responds to certain foods, as well as each person's activity level. To help you balance your diet correctly, you can use an app on your mobile device or online. See Resources on page 154 for apps that can help you balance your diet to optimize it for ketosis.

Reducing the amount of carbohydrates in your diet doesn't mean that you can't eat the things you love—you just need to consume them smartly and in moderation. While we all need carbohydrates (carbs) for fuel, not all carbs work the same way in our bodies. Some carbs burn quickly, while others burn more slowly.

And that's where the recipes in this book come in. If you love baking and eating baked goods but want to keep eating them while keeping a low-carb profile, you can do it! Here you'll find a range of recipes that use low-carb baking flours, such as nut flours and coconut flour, as well as low-carb sweeteners. Let's talk about these ingredients first, so you can familiarize with what's needed before you begin baking.

LOW-CARB FLOURS

I use almond and coconut flours for the recipes in this book because they have the greatest health benefits of all the low-carb baking flours, they're readily available, and they have distinct characteristics that make them great for baking.

COCONUT FLOUR

When it comes to coconut flour, there's so much to love: it's high in fiber and protein, low in carbohydrates, and gluten-free. It's made from the fiber-rich dried coconut that remains after coconut oil is extracted from coconut flesh. A pure, natural, one-ingredient product, it's a healthy alternative to wheat and other gluten-free flours and works well in a wide variety of recipes that call for flour. It's also higher in protein than most gluten-free flours—including oat bran and ground flaxseed—and has about the same protein content as buckwheat and whole wheat flours, making it nutrient-rich while also being wheat-free.

You won't need a lot of flour to bake something with coconut flour, but it does require a binding agent, which usually means at least one or two eggs. It also requires more moisture than usual, so you'll notice that many recipes have added liquid to aid in moistening the batter and the final baked product.

When a cake or other baked item includes coconut flour, I recommend letting the batter sit for a few minutes to give the

STORING COCONUT FLOUR

~∾~

Coconut flour tends to absorb moisture, so it's a good idea to keep it well sealed. If you're not using it within a few weeks, I suggest storing it in the refrigerator and bringing it to room temperature before using it in a recipe.

coconut flour time to absorb the moisture in the batter. You may notice the batter getting a bit thicker after some resting time.

Coconut flour also has the effect of yielding lighter baked goods because it is not as heavy as nut flour. A little bit goes a much longer way, with great-tasting results.

COCONUT FLOUR: BETTER FOR BLOOD SUGAR

Blood sugar (also referred to as blood glucose) is the amount of glucose in our blood, which we rely on for energy. Blood sugar increases after we eat, and our bodies respond to the increase by releasing a hormone called *insulin* to control the level of sugar in our blood so that it doesn't get too high. A rapid drop in blood sugar, on the other hand, is controlled by a hormone, which stimulates the release of more sugar in our blood. This balancing of blood sugar is at play all the time and especially after we eat.

Because the carbohydrates we eat are broken down into glucose, they have a greater effect on our blood sugar. Food and meals that are high in carbohydrates, for example,

can cause a rapid rise in blood sugar, which forces your body to respond. This sudden rise stresses the body as the pancreas pumps a large amount of insulin to manage the rush of blood sugar. Over time, high blood sugar levels can lead to or complicate various health issues, including diabetes, heart disease, and hypoglycemia, and can affect weight gain and overall health.

Fortunately, coconut flour helps keep our blood sugar at a healthy level thanks to its high fiber content. The fiber in coconut flour is low in digestible carbohydrates, so it doesn't have the same effect on our blood sugar compared to other carbohydrates such as wheat grains, and rice. To give you an idea of how high in fiber it is, coconut flour has four times the amount of fiber as oat bran and two times that of wheat bran! As this fiber goes through the digestive system, it helps digest food, makes us feel full, and cleans out other residue before leaving our bodies.

ALMOND FLOUR AND OTHER NUT FLOURS

Almond flour and other nut flours, such as cashew and pecan, have the same benefits as coconut flour—they are low in carbohydrates and help keep blood sugar at a healthy level.

Almond flour, or blanched almond flour, is finely ground, raw, blanched almonds. Blanched almonds have had their skins removed. I prefer blanched almond flour because it has a mild flavor and can be purchased in a very finely ground state. Baking with it imparts a texture similar to all-purpose flour. It's one of my favorite low-carb flours, both for its flavor and for its texture. It tastes great in baked goods such as cookies, cakes, muffins, and pie crusts.

When measuring almond flour and other nut flours, I use the scoop and sweep method; however, you can also measure by weight. I provide both volume and weight measurements in my recipes so you can use the method you prefer.

I use this conversion for almond flour: ½ cup almond flour = 48 grams.

ALMOND FLOUR: HIGH IN PROTEIN AND GOOD FATS

Almond flour is higher in protein and mono-unsaturated fats (the same type of healthy fats found in olive oil) than most low-carb flours. In addition, almonds contain healthy amounts of vitamin E, potassium, and magnesium.

While you can make almond flour at home, I much prefer buying finely ground blanched almond flour because it is invariably more fine and uniform in texture than what I can produce at home. While it's cheaper to buy almond flour in bulk, it also has a shorter shelf life than regular flour, so if you're not using it often, store it in the refrigerator. See resources (page 154) for more information on where to purchase almond and other nut flours.

CASHEW FLOUR

Cashew flour is most often made from raw cashews as opposed to roasted cashews. You can make it yourself by grinding raw cashews in a food processor or high-speed blender with a dry blade (such as a Vitamix) to make a fine flour. Just be careful not to overgrind the flour into nut butter.

HAZELNUT FLOUR

Hazelnut flour is made from ground-up roasted hazelnuts and is easy to make at home (and usually less expensive). The nuts must

ALMOND FLOUR VS. ALMOND MEAL

〜✕〜

Not to be confused with blanched almond flour, almond meal is ground-up almonds with the skins left on instead of blanched off. Almond meal works well in hardier or more rustic recipes and has a slightly more grainy texture because of the skins.

HOW TO REMOVE THE SKINS FROM HAZELNUTS

〜✕〜

To remove the skins from hazelnuts (also referred to as filberts), preheat your oven to 300°F (150°C, or gas mark 2). Spread the hazelnuts in a single layer across a rimmed baking sheet and toast for 10 minutes. Remove the hazelnuts from the oven and let cool. Place the nuts in a towel and rub to remove as much of the skins as possible. Don't worry if you can't get all of the skins off; what comes off easily is enough.

first be roasted and cooled, then skinned (see previous page) and ground. Store any excess flour in the freezer, as nut flours tend to go rancid more quickly than other flours.

PECAN FLOUR

Pecan flour is ground-up roasted pecans. It goes well in recipes for hardy muffins, sweet breads, pancakes, and waffles. To make it at home, place toasted and cooled pecans in a food processor or dry high-speed blender and pulse until the pecans become a fine flour. Store any excess flour in the freezer.

LOW-CARB SWEETENERS

There are a variety of low-carb sweeteners you can use in your baking. You can use one type of low-carb sweetener or a combination of low-carb sweeteners.

Your choice of sweetener will most likely come down to the taste you prefer as well as the other ingredients in the recipe. Each low-carb sweetener has distinct characteristics. Some are better used in baking, while others can be used in almost all recipes. To help you compare common low-carb sweeteners, I created the chart on page 15. See also the resources section on page 154, for brand names of each type of sweetener.

I tested the recipes in this book using Swerve, which is a combination of erythritol and oligosaccharides. Erythritol is commonly used because it can easily be substituted in an equal amount for the sugar in a recipe.

Swerve and other sweeteners sometimes have what is referred to as a "cooling" taste. You can reduce this effect by using erythritol and stevia in a 3:1 ratio, respectively.

SWEETENERS WITH BULK

Low-carb sweeteners can be divided into two categories: those that have "bulk" and those that don't. Sweeteners that have bulk add to the volume and weight of a recipe, as well as the texture, just like traditional sugar. For example, erythritol and xylitol have bulk, so they will be good when sweetening an item such as a cake or a cupcake.

Stevia and monk fruit are not bulk sweeteners, so they can be used to sweeten a recipe without adding volume or weight to it. They don't measure like sugar and are not measured in equal amounts to replace sugar. For example, stevia is much sweeter than sugar, so only a few drops are used. The same goes for monk fruit: you only need a small amount to replace a cup of sugar.

To determine which sweeteners are best to use in recipes, refer to the Low-Carb Sweetener Conversion Chart on page 15, as well as the manufacturer's conversion recommendations.

All the recipes in this book are based on a 1:1 conversion for sugar, so you'll want to use an alternative sweetener that can be substituted in equal parts (1:1) for sugar. For example, when baking the Cinnamon Bun Muffins on page 61, which call for "½ cup low-carb sweetener (1:1)," you'll want to use a

ALMOND FLOUR VS. ALMOND MEAL

∽⌐∾

Not to be confused with blanched almond flour, almond meal is ground up almonds with the skins left on instead of blanched off. Almond meal works well in hardier or more rustic recipes and has a slightly more grainy texture because of the skins.

CALCULATING NET CARBS

∽⌐∾

I've added a nutrition analysis for each recipe, which lists, among other things, the total carbohydrates (carbs) per serving, or carbs from both fiber and sugar. What isn't included is the *net carb* amount, which is different from the *total carb* amount. Net carbs are calculated by taking the total carbs and subtracting the fiber and sugar alcohols (found in low-carb sweeteners). Depending on what low-carb sweetener you use, this sugar alcohol content will vary, so it's impossible to calculate net carbs until you know what sweetener you're using and how much. Erythritol, monk fruit, and stevia contribute very little net carbs to recipes, so these low-carb sweeteners will keep the net carbs low. Look online for more resources on calculating net carbs if you would like to do so once you have all your sweeteners selected.

sweetener that has bulk and can be substituted 1:1 for sugar, such as Swerve, Lakanto, or erythritol. If you prefer to use erythritol plus stevia instead of ½ cup of Swerve, remember that these sweeteners don't measure in the same 1:1 ratio, so you'll want to change it to ¼ cup erythritol plus 1 teaspoon powdered stevia extract. In such cases, it's best to refer to the chart on the opposite page or to the conversion instructions on the box itself for calculating how much to use. For a smoothie, instead of using 1 tablespoon of bulk sweetener, you can use the equivalent number of stevia drops the manufacturer recommends to substitute for 1 tablespoon of sugar.

GOOD OILS AND FATS

Oils are obtained by pressing oil-rich plants to release their oils. Oils that I like to use and that you'll see in this book include olive oil, nut and seed oils, and coconut oil. I try

to stick with those that are minimally processed, so I look for words like "cold-pressed" and "unrefined." I do also use refined oils on occasion, but only for high-heat cooking and only from trusted brands and sources, such as Spectrum Organics. I also use butter and ghee, organic and from grass-fed animals whenever possible.

I don't mind spending a little extra money on healthy fats and oils that are minimally processed and from reliable sources because the fats they contain are essential to good

LOW-CARB SWEETENER CONVERSION CHART

SWEETENER	1 CUP SUGAR =	GOOD FOR . . .	NOTES
STEVIA (POWDERED)	½ to 1 teaspoon	Jams, frostings, glazes, beverages	• Derived from a plant • Much sweeter than sugar, so a little goes a long way • No bulk • Has an aftertaste
STEVIA (LIQUID)	1 to 2 teaspoons	Jams, frostings, glazes, beverages	• Derived from a plant • Much sweeter than sugar, so a little goes a long way • No bulk • Has an aftertaste
LAKANTO (ERYTHRITOL + MONK FRUIT)	1 cup	Baking	• Brand-name product • Naturally occurring sugar alcohol derived from fruit • Has bulk • Caramelizes
ERYTHRITOL	1¼ cups	Baking, most often combined with a few drops of stevia at a ratio of 75% erythritol to 25% stevia.	• Sugar alcohol derived from plants, occurs naturally in fruits and fungi • About 70% as sweet as sugar, so use an extra ¼ to ⅓ more than sugar • Typically combined with other low-carb sweeteners • Has a grainy taste • Caramelizes when heated • Can cause digestive issues • Has a cooling sensation • Has bulk
XYLITOL	1 cup	Baking, frosting, and glazes in small amounts	• Sugar alcohol derived from plants • Poisonous to dogs • Used in toothpaste and shown to prevent cavities • Can cause digestive issues • Has bulk
SWERVE (ERYTHRITOL AND OLIGOSACCHARIDES)	1 cup	Baking, jams, frostings, glazes	• Brand-name product • Tastes like sugar • Measures like sugar • Has bulk

health and help our bodies absorb and process fat-soluble minerals and vitamins. While I use both dairy-based and dairy-free fats in my cooking, you can easily bake and cook dairy-free using just coconut oil and other plant-based oils and fats.

That said, it is important to keep in mind the smoke point of various oils when cooking and baking. For high-heat applications, I avoid using oils that smoke or burn at a lower temperature, such as olive oil, butter, and many unrefined oils. The oils that can be used at cooking and baking temperatures above 350°F (180°C, or gas mark 4) include refined coconut oil, ghee, and high-heat cooking oil. Look at your labels (they should say) if you're unsure of your oil's smoke point, and be sure to stay under that mark when heating.

MILKS AND CREAMS

There's a variety of creams and milks that can be used in the recipes in this book. Some are dairy-based and some are dairy-free. Many of the dairy-free milks, such as coconut, hazelnut, and almond milk, are subtly sweet, making them a nice substitute for dairy-based milks.

My favorite dairy-free milks are almond and coconut milk. I recommend choosing brands without additives and thickening agents. It's fairly easy to make them from scratch if you have the time (see next page); you just need to have some raw almonds or unsweetened shredded coconut on hand (see resources, page 154).

If you have no need to avoid dairy, feel free to use regular milk in any recipe that calls for dairy-free milk, unless noted otherwise. Likewise, if you do need to avoid dairy, sub in dairy-free milk.

In many of the recipes that call for milk, you can also use heavy cream, yogurt, or sour cream to produce an even richer baked result. For dairy-free whipped cream, you can make Coconut Whipped Cream (page 100).

HOMEMADE COCONUT MILK

I find it convenient to whip up a small amount of coconut milk when I'm out of store-bought or just need a little bit of milk and don't want to open a whole container or can. You can make this in a matter of minutes if you're rushed for time, whereas almond milk requires about 8 hours of soaking time.

1 cup (64 g) unsweetened shredded coconut (see resources, page 154)

2 cups (475 ml) water

1. Combine the coconut and water in a blender container and let soak for about 2 hours. Or, if you're short on time, soak the coconut in hot water (about the temperature of hot tap water) for a few minutes and move on to the next step.

2. Blend in a high-speed blender on the highest speed for a minute or two.

3. Strain the coconut milk through several layers of cheesecloth or a nut milk bag into a pitcher or bowl; discard the solids. Store the milk in the refrigerator. It will keep for several days.

YIELD: 2 cups (475 ml)

HOMEMADE ALMOND MILK

Almond milk is a naturally sweet, dairy-free milk that can be used in place of any other milk in the recipes in this book. All you need are almonds, water, and a bit of preplanning.

1 cup (145 g) raw almonds

2 cups (475 ml) water

1. Place the almonds in a bowl and cover them with water. Soak overnight or for at least 8 to 10 hours.

2. Drain and rinse the almonds and place them in a high-speed blender. Add the 2 cups (475 ml) water and blend until the almonds are completely ground up; I blend mine for about 1 minute.

3. Strain the almond milk through a nut milk bag or several layers of cheesecloth into a pitcher or bowl; discard the solids. Store the milk in the refrigerator. It will keep for several days.

YIELD: 2 cups (475 ml)

OTHER SUBSTITUTIONS

Substituting ingredients successfully can vary from recipe to recipe. You'll want to take into account how swapping out one ingredient for another will affect the overall taste and texture of a dish. Some recipes in this book are flexible enough that you can substitute one ingredient for another, such as dairy-free milk for regular milk, as mentioned above. I've made a note in those recipes where substitutions were tested and are possible. If there are other substitutions you are keen on making, read through the following tips and techniques—and note that results may vary!

REPLACING EGGS

The egg is a tricky ingredient to swap out because it is a flavorless, and often vital, binding agent used in most of the recipes in this book, especially the recipes that use coconut flour. Still, there are few substitutions you can make.

FLAXSEED MEAL

You can substitute one or two flaxseed eggs for regular eggs in most muffin, cupcake, and bread recipes. Flaxseed meal is ground flaxseeds and can be used as a moist binding agent in place of up to two eggs. I keep a small amount of flaxseeds in my refrigerator and place them in a coffee or spice grinder to grind them into meal as needed. In general,

I recommend using only one or at most two flaxseed eggs, and it also depends on the other recipe ingredients.

To create a flaxseed egg, use this ratio: 1 tablespoon (7 g) flaxseed meal + 3 tablespoons (45 ml) water = 1 egg

BAKING SODA AND VINEGAR

Baking soda plus vinegar can also be used to replace eggs, although I've found this technique to be less reliable than the other substitutes, so proceed with caution. Add the baking soda to the dry ingredients in the recipe and add the vinegar to the wet ingredients, then combine the dry and wet ingredients. A chemical reaction will release gas and lift your batter. Place the batter in the oven as soon as you combine the dry and wet ingredients, before the gas can escape.

To create a baking soda and vinegar egg, use this ratio: 1 teaspoon (4.6 g) baking soda + 1 teaspoon (5 ml) apple cider vinegar = 1 egg

BAKING TIPS

There are a few things about low-carb baking that are good to know before you get started. Knowing the "personality" of flours like coconut and almond flour is imperative for baking success! And, just like traditional baking, be sure to bring eggs and milk to room temperature for best results.

To get a good fitting circle of parchment paper for the inside of a cake or bread pan, trace the pan on the parchment paper and then cut out the traced shape. I often grease the inside of the pan and then place the cutout paper in the pan. Once the cake or bread is baked, you can remove it more easily because the bottom won't stick! Or you can just leave the paper in until you're finished using the pan.

LET'S GET STARTED!

Baking and cooking is a fun adventure with great rewards at the finish line. But before you dive in, just remember my final few tips: bring ingredients to room temperature before beginning, read the recipe at least once before starting, and don't be afraid to get messy. All recipes found in this cookbook are grain-free and gluten-free. Eat well, be well, and enjoy it too!

HOW TO MAKE PARCHMENT LINERS

Parchment liners for cupcakes and muffins are a fun way to make your baked goods even more enticing. To make liners, cut a large sheet of parchment paper into 5-inch (13 cm) squares. Lightly grease your muffin or cupcake pan and press a parchment square into each cup, folding and overlapping along the creases. Carefully pour the batter into each liner and bake as directed. Serve with the liners on for a nice presentation and easy packaging.

CHAPTER 2

BREADS, BISCUITS, AND PIZZA

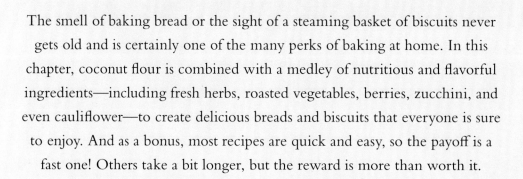

The smell of baking bread or the sight of a steaming basket of biscuits never gets old and is certainly one of the many perks of baking at home. In this chapter, coconut flour is combined with a medley of nutritious and flavorful ingredients—including fresh herbs, roasted vegetables, berries, zucchini, and even cauliflower—to create delicious breads and biscuits that everyone is sure to enjoy. And as a bonus, most recipes are quick and easy, so the payoff is a fast one! Others take a bit longer, but the reward is more than worth it.

EVERYDAY POPOVERS

· DAIRY-FREE · NUT-FREE ·GRAIN-FREE ·GLUTEN-FREE

Popovers are the American variation of English Yorkshire Pudding. This recipe yields popovers that are just as you'd expect. They're light, almost hollow, and easy to make at a moment's notice. You can add a variety of additions depending on your taste; I've included both a savory and a sweet popover recipe following this basic one to give you some ideas. Just note that you'll want to bake the popovers in nonstick popover sleeves, parchment paper, or muffin liners. See page 22 on how to make your own liners.

4 large eggs

½ cup (120 ml) coconut milk or other milk

⅛ teaspoon salt

2 tablespoons (13 g) coconut flour

1. Preheat your oven to 425°F (220°C, or gas mark 7).

2. Add all the ingredients to a bowl and whisk until fully blended and a bit bubbly. The batter will have a liquid consistency.

3. Fill muffin liners or nonstick popover sleeves about two-thirds of the way with batter.

4. Bake for 15 minutes, or until they begin to brown on top, keeping the oven door closed to prevent them from collapsing.

5. Cool for a moment and serve. These are best served soon after they come out of the oven, but can be kept covered and warm for a while as well.

YIELD: 6 popovers

PER SERVING: 45 calories; 1 g carbohydrate; 3 g fat; 3 g protein; 1 g fiber

PARMESAN-THYME POPOVERS

•NUT-FREE   •GRAIN-FREE   •GLUTEN-FREE

A combination of herbs and aged cheese makes for a light, savory roll that is the perfect accompaniment to any meal, soup, or stew. You can replace the Parmesan with another hard or soft cheese such as Pecorino or Cheddar, or try adding pesto, garlic, chives, and other herbs to create your favorite mix.

4 large eggs

½ cup (120 ml) coconut milk or other milk

2 tablespoons (13 g) coconut flour

Pinch salt (less than ⅛ teaspoon)

1 tablespoon (5 g) grated Parmesan cheese

1 tablespoon (2.4 g) chopped fresh thyme

1. Preheat your oven to 425°F (220°C, or gas mark 7).

2. Add all the ingredients to a bowl and whisk until fully blended and a bit bubbly. The batter will have a liquid consistency.

3. Fill muffin liners or nonstick popover sleeves one-half to two-thirds of the way with batter.

4. Bake for about 15 minutes, or until they begin to brown on top, keeping the oven door closed to prevent them from collapsing.

5. Cool for a moment and serve. These are best served soon after they come out of the oven, but can be kept covered and warm for a while as well.

YIELD: 6 popovers

PER SERVING: 64 calories; 2 g carbohydrate; 34g fat; 3 g protein; 1 g fiber

SANDWICH BREAD

•DAIRY-FREE   •NUT-FREE OPTION   •GRAIN-FREE   •GLUTEN-FREE

This is an easy-to-bake bread that can be used for sandwiches, rolls, and toast. What's also nice about it is its overall texture, which tastes like sandwich bread that contains gluten. It stays together well, and it's a bit firm on the outside and softer on the inside.

This is also a very flexible recipe, in that you can use just about any nut or seed butter. The flavor and color may change a bit, but the overall texture stays the same. If the nut butter is dark, like roasted almond butter, the bread will be on the darker side, while the opposite is true for lighter butters, such as cashew. Double the recipe to make more than one loaf at a time.

To make it nut-free, use sunflower seed butter or pumpkin seed butter.

¾ cup (195 g) smooth nut butter (almond or cashew)

4 eggs

1 tablespoon low-carb 1:1 sweetener, or equivalent (see chart on page 15)

¼ cup (24 g) finely ground nut flour (blanched almond or cashew flour)

¼ teaspoon baking soda

¼ teaspoon salt

1. Preheat your oven to 350°F (175°C, or gas mark 4).

2. In a large mixing bowl, use a spatula or mixer to blend together the nut butter, eggs, and sweetener until creamy.

3. Add the remaining dry ingredients to the batter and blend until creamy.

4. Pour the batter into a baking pan; I use a 7.5×3.5×2.25-inch (19×9×7 cm) loaf pan, but you can use a larger pan.

5. Bake for 40 minutes, or until a toothpick inserted into the center of the loaf comes out clean.

6. Cool and slice. Store in the refrigerator for a few weeks, or in the freezer for a month or so.

YIELD: 1 loaf, 8 servings

PER SERVING: 198 calories; 5 g carbohydrate; 16 g fat; 8 g protein; 1 g fiber

CAULIFLOWER PIZZA CRUST

·NUT-FREE   ·GRAIN-FREE   ·GLUTEN-FREE

Creating a pizza crust using cauliflower requires a few more steps than other grain-free, gluten-free pizza crusts, but the flavor and texture of this pizza is worth the extra effort. It's the kind of crust that's tender and thick, like a deep-dish or thick, doughy crust, thanks in part to the delicious cheese that accompanies the cauliflower.

2 cups (232 g) grated cauliflower florets (about 1 medium cauliflower head)

1 medium garlic clove, peeled and pressed or finely minced

¼ teaspoon salt

2 teaspoons (1.5 g) chopped fresh herbs (oregano, basil, rosemary, or other)

1 egg

2 tablespoons (13 g) coconut flour

½ cup (44 g) grated Parmesan cheese or other cheese, or a mix of grated hard and soft cheeses

1. Preheat your oven to 450°F (230°C, or gas mark 8).

2. Line baking sheets with parchment paper or other nonstick material.

3. Place the cauliflower florets in a food processor and pulse until the florets are finely riced. Alternatively, you can grate the florets using a box or cheese grater.

4. Prepare a steamer and steam the riced cauliflower for, about 5 minutes, or until it is just tender but not soft throughout.

5. Remove excess moisture from the steamed riced cauliflower by placing it in a nut milk bag, cheesecloth, or dish towel and squeezing it over the sink. If the cauliflower is hot, wear dish-washing gloves when doing this step. The more moisture you can remove, the better your pizza will be.

6. Add the cauliflower, garlic, salt, herbs, egg, coconut flour, and cheese to a mixing bowl and blend well.

7. On parchment paper or a nonstick surface, shape the mixture into two small circles, or one large circle or square, about ½ inch (1.3 cm) thick. The dough is fairly loose, so use your hands to shape and flatten it.

8. Bake the pizza crust for about 10 minutes, or until the edges begin to brown. Now you can add toppings and bake for another 5 minutes, or you can store the crusts in a sealed container in the refrigerator for a few days or in the freezer for a few months.

YIELD: 1 large or 2 small pizza crusts, 8 servings

PER SERVING: 121 calories; 2 g carbohydrate; 8 g fat; 11 g protein; 1 g fiber

GARLIC-CAULIFLOWER BREADSTICKS

·NUT-FREE   ·GRAIN-FREE   ·GLUTEN-FREE

When you're in the mood for pizza-style breadsticks with marinara sauce and cheese, but without the extra carbohydrates that come from grain-based crusts, you'll be happy you have this in your repertoire. Cauliflower lends itself well to yielding a thick, soft crust, be it in pizza or breadstick form—you'll be amazed that it's completely grain-free!

2 cups (232 g) grated cauliflower

½ cup (44 g) grated Parmesan cheese or other cheese, or a mix of hard and soft cheeses, divided

1 garlic clove, peeled and pressed or finely minced

¼ teaspoon salt

2 teaspoons chopped fresh herbs (oregano, basil, rosemary, or other), or 1 teaspoon dried herbs

1 egg

2 tablespoons (13 g) coconut flour

½ cup (125 g) marinara sauce (or Tomato Chutney, page 152)

1. Preheat your oven to 450°F (230°C, or gas mark 8) and line a baking sheet with parchment paper.

2. Place the cauliflower florets in a food processor and pulse until the florets are finely riced. Alternatively, you can grate the florets using a box or cheese grater.

3. Prepare a steamer and steam the riced cauliflower for about 5 minutes until tender, but not soft.

4. Remove excess moisture from the steamed riced cauliflower by adding it to a nut milk bag, cheesecloth, or dish towel and squeezing it over the sink. If the cauliflower is hot, wear dishwashing gloves to protect your hands.

5. Add the cauliflower, ¼ cup (22 g) of the cheese, garlic, salt, herbs, egg, and coconut flour in a mixing bowl and blend well.

6. On parchment paper or a nonstick surface, shape the mixture into a rectangle about ½ inch (1.3 cm) thick.

7. Bake the breadsticks for 15 minutes, or until the edges begin to brown. Brush the top of the dough with marinara sauce and sprinkle the remaining ¼ cup (22 g) cheese evenly across the sauce. Place back in the oven and bake until the cheese starts to brown.

8. Cool for a minute, slice, and serve warm. Store sealed in the refrigerator for a few days or freeze for a few months.

YIELD: 16 breadsticks

PER SERVING: 63 calories; 1 g carbohydrate; 4 g fat; 5 g protein; 1 g fiber

EVERYDAY FLATBREAD

·GRAIN-FREE   ·GLUTEN-FREE

This flatbread can be used for a thin crust pizza or as bread for dipping in soups, sauces, and stews. I've used a variety of cheeses with this recipe, including mozzarella, Parmesan, aged sheep's and aged goat's milk cheese.

2 cups (192 g) almond flour

2 tablespoons (13 g) coconut flour

½ teaspoon salt

½ teaspoon baking soda

¼ cup (60 ml) olive oil or other oil

4 large eggs

1 cup (115 g) shredded mozzarella or other cheese

1. Preheat your oven to 350°F (175°C, or gas mark 4).

2. Place the almond flour, coconut flour, salt, and baking soda in a bowl and whisk with a fork.

3. Add the oil, eggs, and cheese to the flour mixture and blend well. The dough will be slightly wet.

4. Shape the dough into one or two balls using your hands. Cover the dough and place it in the freezer for 10 minutes first. Cut two large pieces of parchment paper and place a dough ball between them. Flatten the dough a bit with your hands and then use a rolling pin to roll the dough flat until it is about ¼ inch (6 mm) thick or to your desired thickness.

5. Remove the top parchment paper and slide the rolled bread and bottom parchment paper onto a baking sheet.

6. Bake for 15 minutes, or until the edges are just starting to brown. Remove from the oven to cool.

7. Slice and serve warm or at room temperature. Store flatbread in a sealed container at room temperature for a few days, in the refrigerator for about a week, or in the freezer for a few months.

YIELD: 2 flatbreads, or about 4 servings

PER SERVING: 370 calories; 6 g carbohydrate; 32 g fat; 16 g protein; 3 g fiber

EVERYDAY NUT-FREE FLATBREAD

•NUT-FREE •GRAIN-FREE •GLUTEN-FREE

This simple nut-free flatbread can be topped with herbs, sauces, and other pizza-style toppings, or just use it as sliced wedges of bread to dip in sauces, stews, and salads. For a focaccia-style topping, try a sprinkle of coarse salt, chopped fresh rosemary, and Roasted Cherry Tomatoes (page 153).

¼ cup (26 g) coconut flour

⅛ teaspoon salt

4 large eggs

1 cup (80 g) shredded Parmesan, or mozzarella (115 g), or other cheese

1 tablespoon (15 ml) olive oil

1. Preheat your oven to 375°F (190°C, or gas mark 5).

2. Line a baking sheet with parchment paper or nonstick mat.

3. Place the coconut flour and salt in a bowl and blend with a fork or whisk.

4. Add the eggs, cheese, and olive oil to the coconut flour mixture and blend well with a spoon or spatula. The dough will be wet.

5. Using a spatula or spoon, spread the dough out into one or two flatbreads that are about ¼ inch (6 mm) thick, or the thickness you prefer.

6. Bake for 15 minutes. If you're adding toppings, bake the bread for only 10 minutes, add the toppings, and continue baking for another 5 to 10 minutes, depending on your toppings.

7. Slice and serve warm or at room temperature. Store in a sealed container at room temperature for a few days, in the refrigerator for about a week, or in the freezer for a few months.

YIELD: 1 large or 2 small flatbreads, or 4 servings

PER SERVING: 211 calories; 4 g carbohydrate; 15 g fat; 15 g protein; 3 g fiber

PESTO FLATBREAD PIZZA

'GRAIN-FREE   'GLUTEN-FREE

Flatbread can have any combination of toppings you desire, so take this list of ingredients as one option. One of my favorite topping combination is Roasted Cherry Tomatoes (page 153) and pesto (recipe follows). If you don't have roasted tomatoes, use either sundried tomatoes or tomato sauce. The pesto recipe is dairy-free but, if you prefer, you can replace the pine nuts and ¼ teaspoon salt with 3 tablespoons (15 g) grated Parmesan. You can also replace the basil with fresh arugula, kale, parsley, oregano, or other mixture of fresh herbs.

1 recipe Everyday Flatbread (page 32), or Everyday Nut-free Flatbread (page 33)

FOR THE PESTO:

1 cup (20 g) packed fresh basil leaves

1 large garlic clove

3 tablespoons (25 g) pine nuts

¼ teaspoon salt

3 tablespoons (45 ml) olive oil

1 teaspoon lemon juice

FOR THE TOPPING:

1 cup (115 g) shredded mozzarella or other cheese

1 cup (150 g) Roasted Cherry Tomatoes (page 153), sundried tomatoes (110 g), or tomato sauce (245 g)

1. Preheat your oven to 400°F (200°C, or gas mark 6). Place prepared flatbread on a baking sheet.

2. **To make the pesto:** Place all the pesto ingredients in a food processor or blender and pulse until well blended.

3. Spread a thin layer of pesto on flatbread.

4. **To make the topping:** Sprinkle the cheese over the pesto, and then layer the tomatoes on top of the cheese.

5. Bake for 5 minutes, or until the cheese is as bubbly and golden as you like.

6. Cool for a moment and slice. Store pizza in a sealed container in the refrigerator for about a week or in the freezer for a few months.

YIELD: 2 flatbread pizzas, or 4 servings

PER SERVING: 270 calories; 5 g carbohydrate; 22 g fat; 16 g protein; 4 g fiber

TORTILLAS

•NUT-FREE   •DAIRY-FREE OPTION   •GRAIN-FREE   •GLUTEN-FREE

Tortillas present endless meal possibilities. I use them in the Roasted Tomato and Pepper Jack Quesadillas (page 144), the Chili-Lime Chicken Quesadillas (page 143), and Mexican Lasagna (page 149). You can also let your imagination run with your favorite fillings and toppings.

Two tips to prevent these tortillas from falling apart: First, be a bit generous with the cooking oil in the skillet; and second, let them brown on the bottom and edges so it is easy to slip a spatula completely under them to flip. A little brown on the bottom is a good thing for these tortillas, and they hold together better the longer they're cooked.

For the egg whites, I usually purchase a container of organic egg whites to make a large batch of tortillas. Then I wrap the tortillas and store them in the refrigerator to have with meals during the week.

⅔ cup (155 ml) egg whites (about 4 large egg whites)

2 tablespoons (28 g) unsalted butter, melted, or ghee or coconut oil, plus more for the skillet

¼ cup (60 ml) coconut milk or other milk

1 tablespoon (15 ml) lime juice

2 tablespoons (13 g) coconut flour

¼ teaspoon ground cumin

¼ teaspoon salt

1. In a bowl, whisk together the egg whites, 2 tablespoons (28 g) unsalted butter, milk, and lime juice.

2. Add the coconut flour, cumin, and salt to the bowl and whisk until well blended. Let the batter sit for a few minutes and mix once more.

3. Heat a skillet over medium heat and add about 2 tablespoons (28 g) unsalted butter, depending on the size of your skillet. One of the tricks to successfully making these is to always have a good layer of oil or butter in the skillet.

4. Pour about 2 tablespoons (28 ml) of batter into the skillet to make a 5-inch (13 cm) tortilla; adjust the amount of batter to make the size you prefer. Tilt the pan in a circular motion to spread the batter around in a circle.

5. Cook for a few minutes, or until the tortilla's edges and bottom are browning and you can easily slip a spatula under it, then flip the tortilla to the other side. Cook for another minute or so and transfer to a warm plate. Repeat with the remaining batter.

6. Serve warm. Store in a sealed container in the refrigerator for a few days or in the freezer for a few months.

YIELD: 6 tortillas

PER SERVING: 53 calories; 2 g carbohydrate; 4 g fat; 1 g protein; 1 g fiber

NO-CORN CORNBREAD

·DAIRY-FREE OPTION   ·GRAIN-FREE   ·GLUTEN-FREE

If you enjoy cornbread but have avoided it because, well, the carbs, I have a treat for you. Here is a recipe for cornbread that doesn't use corn. This recipe can also be doubled for a taller cornbread. If you double it, bake it for another 5 to 10 minutes, or until a toothpick inserted into the center comes out clean.

To make it dairy-free, use coconut oil instead of butter, and use a dairy-free milk such as coconut or almond milk. See resources on page 154 for milk brands. And if you really want to change things up, replace some of the butter with bacon grease and bake it in a cast-iron skillet, also rubbed with bacon grease.

I use an 8×8-inch (20×20 cm), baking dish lined with parchment paper, and the bread is about 1 inch (2.5 cm) in thickness. To get thicker bread, use a smaller baking pan or double the recipe and use a larger baking dish.

½ cup (48 g) almond flour

¼ cup (26 g) coconut flour

¼ teaspoon salt

¼ teaspoon baking soda

3 large eggs

¼ cup (55 g) unsalted butter

2 tablespoons low-carb 1:1 sweetener, or equivalent (see chart on page 15)

½ cup (120 ml) coconut milk or other milk

1. Preheat your oven to 325°F (170°C, or gas mark 3).

2. Line an 8×8-inch (20×20 cm) baking dish or cast-iron skillet with parchment paper or other nonstick covering, or grease well.

3. Mix all the dry ingredients in a bowl until well blended.

4. Add all the wet ingredients to the dry ingredients and blend well.

5. Pour the batter into the baking pan and bake for 20 minutes, or until a toothpick inserted into the center of the bread comes out clean.

6. Cool and slice. Store in the refrigerator for a week or so, or freeze for a few months.

YIELD: 6 to 8 servings

PER SERVING: 65 calories; 2 g carbohydrate; 6 g fat; 2 g protein; 1 g fiber

BISCUITS

·EGG-FREE   ·DAIRY-FREE OPTION   ·GRAIN-FREE   ·GLUTEN-FREE

These biscuits have a great texture and flavor thanks to the almond flour. Eat them with butter or jelly, with a meal, or with hot soup. Or alone, straight out of the oven. For a dairy-free version, substitute coconut oil for the butter. If you don't need to be dairy-free but want to avoid milk solids, use ghee in place of butter.

2½ cups (240 g) almond flour

½ teaspoon salt

½ teaspoon baking soda

¼ cup (56 g) unsalted butter, softened

1 tablespoon low-carb 1:1 sweetener, or equivalent (see chart on page 15)

1. Combine all the dry ingredients in a bowl and blend well with a fork or spatula.

2. In another bowl, whisk the wet ingredients and then combine them with the dry ingredients.

3. Blend well with a fork and roll the dough into a ball.

4. Place the dough in the freezer for about 10 minutes.

5. Preheat your oven to 350°F (175°C, or gas mark 4).

6. Prepare a baking sheet with a nonstick baking mat or parchment paper.

7. Take the dough out of the freezer and place it between 2 pieces of parchment paper or other nonstick materials. Roll it to a thickness of about 1 inch (2.5 cm) and cut the biscuits out with a 4-inch (10.2 cm) cookie cutter. Re-roll the scraps and cut out more biscuits. Alternatively, you can roll small balls of dough in your hand and then flatten them to about 1 inch (2.5 cm) thick.

8. Place the biscuits on the baking sheet and bake for 12 minutes, or until they're browned on the edges and a toothpick inserted into the center comes out clean.

YIELD: 6 to 8 servings

PER SERVING: 167 calories; 3 g carbohydrate; 16 g fat; 5 g protein; 3 g fiber

DROP BISCUITS

•DAIRY-FREE OPTION   •NUT-FREE   •GRAIN-FREE   •GLUTEN-FREE

You might think it unreasonable to get tender, savory biscuits using coconut flour, but add the right amount of moisture and butter and it's biscuits and gravy time. This basic biscuit recipe can accompany a soup or stew, or you can just snack on them with a smear of jam or butter (omit herbs if so).

You can use any kind of milk in this recipe, dairy or dairy-free, or make it richer by trying cream, sour cream, or yogurt instead of the milk. And if you're finding these biscuits a bit on the dry side, add another tablespoon of milk or even water

4 eggs

¼ cup (57 g) unsalted butter, melted, or coconut oil

1¼ cups (300 ml) coconut milk or other milk

¼ teaspoon salt

¼ teaspoon baking soda

²/₃ cup (70 g) coconut flour

1 tablespoon (2.5 g) chopped fresh herbs such as basil, oregano, parsley, or thyme (optional)

1. Preheat your oven to 350°F (180°C, or gas mark 4).

2. Generously grease a baking sheet, or line it with parchment paper or a nonstick mat.

3. Using a whisk or handheld mixer, mix together the eggs, butter, milk, salt, baking soda, and herbs until well blended.

4. Add the coconut flour to the batter and mix until well blended and free of lumps. Let the batter sit for a few minutes and mix again. The batter should be mushy and easy to spoon and drop onto the baking sheet. If you find it's too stiff, add another tablespoon of coconut milk or water.

5. Spoon about 2 tablespoons (42 g) of batter for each biscuit onto the greased baking sheet.

6. Bake for 20 minutes or until the biscuits are tender but firm. Serve warm or at room temperature. Store in a sealed container in the refrigerator for a few days or in the freezer for a few months. For leftovers, reheat or toast for a few minutes to serve warm.

YIELD: 12 biscuits

PER SERVING: 71 calories; 4 g carbohydrate; 6 g fat; 1 g protein; 2 g fiber

CHEDDAR BISCUITS

•NUT-FREE   •GRAIN-FREE   •GLUTEN-FREE

This drop biscuit is moist and savory thanks to the cheddar cheese. Cheddar and butter make excellent flavoring for this simple biscuit, and these can be reheated or toasted for a few minutes to serve warm.

4 large eggs

¼ cup (57 g) cup unsalted butter, melted

1¼ cups (300 ml) coconut milk or other milk

¼ teaspoon salt

¼ teaspoon baking soda

¼ teaspoon garlic powder

½ cup (56 g) finely shredded or grated sharp cheddar cheese

1 tablespoon (4 g) fresh oregano, basil, or other herbs (optional)

⅔ cup (70 g) coconut flour

1. Preheat your oven to 350°F (180°C, or gas mark 4).

2. Generously grease a baking sheet, or line it with parchment paper or a nonstick mat.

3. Using a handheld or stand mixer, mix together the eggs, butter, milk, salt, baking soda, garlic powder, cheese, and herbs until well blended.

4. Add the coconut flour to the batter and mix until well blended and all the lumps are gone. Let the batter sit for a few minutes and mix again. The batter should be mushy and easy to spoon and drop onto the baking sheet. If you find it's too stiff, add another tablespoon of coconut milk or water.

5. Spoon about 2 tablespoons (42 g) of batter for each biscuit onto the greased baking sheet.

6. Bake for 25 minutes or until the biscuits are tender but firm.

7. Serve warm or at room temperature. Store in a sealed container in the refrigerator for a few days or in the freezer for a few months. For leftovers, reheat or toast for a few minutes to serve warm.

YIELD: 12 biscuits

PER SERVING: 125 calories; 10 g carbohydrate; 7 g fat; 5 g protein; 3 g fiber

CHOCOLATE ZUCCHINI BREAD

•DAIRY-FREE   •NUT-FREE   •GRAIN-FREE   •GLUTEN-FREE

Here's a chocolate take on zucchini bread. Not too dense, this chocolate zucchini bread is moist, dark, and subtly sweet.

Some of this bread's sweetness comes from sweetened chocolate chips, but if you don't want to add them, it is still sweet on its own. I recommend using a low-carb sweetener that has bulk for this recipe. For low-carb chips, see reources on page 154.

A nice addition is ½ teaspoon of ground cinnamon, and if you want a bit of a kick in the flavor, add ½ teaspoon of chili powder.

This recipe is quite flexible, so feel free to bake it in a loaf pan as a bread, a square baking pan to make cake squares, or a muffin pan to have cupcakes (these will bake a little faster than a bread or cake). It's up to you.

2 cups (200 g) grated or finely shredded zucchini (about 1 zucchini)

4 large eggs

2 tablespoons (30 ml) olive oil, unsalted butter, ghee, or coconut oil

⅓ cup low-carb 1:1 sweetener, or equivalent (see chart on page 15)

1 teaspoon vanilla extract

⅓ cup (35 g) coconut flour

¼ cup (20 g) unsweetened cocoa powder

½ teaspoon baking soda

½ teaspoon salt

⅓ cup (56 g) sugar-free chocolate chips

1. Preheat your oven to 350°F (180°C, or gas mark 4).

2. Grease the baking pan and line the bottom with parchment paper. Dust the sides with coconut flour. If you want easy release, line the entire pan with parchment paper.

3. If your zucchini is too moist, wring out the excess moisture by placing the zucchini in a towel and squeezing.

4. Using a food processor or mixer, blend together the zucchini, eggs, oil, sweetener, and vanilla. A food processor will further break up the zucchini so you won't see it in the baked bread.

5. Add the flour, cocoa, baking soda, and salt to the zucchini mixture and stir until well blended. Let the batter sit for a few minutes.

6. Mix in the chocolate chips, then pour the batter into the prepared pan and bake for 45 to 50 minutes or until a toothpick inserted in the center comes out clean.

7. Cool and serve. Store, covered, at room temperature for several days or in the refrigerator for a few weeks.

YIELD: 1 loaf, or 10 servings

PER SERVING: 149 calories; 17 g carbohydrate; 8 g fat; 4 g protein; 3 g fiber

CHEESY BAGELS

•NUT-FREE   •GRAIN-FREE   •GLUTEN-FREE

This is a fun recipe to work with because, unlike many low-carb bread recipes, it can be formed into a dough ball that is stretchy and can be shaped into bagels with your hands. For the mozzarella, I recommend the unsalted low-moisture shredded version. For a dairy-free bagel, see page 65.

½ cup (52 g) coconut flour

2 teaspoons baking powder

12 ounces (340 g) low-moisture shredded mozzarella cheese

2 large eggs

2 tablespoons (about 12 g) bagel topping (poppy seeds, sesame seeds, salt, or other topping; optional)

1. Preheat your oven to 350°F (175°C, or gas mark 4).

2. Prepare a baking sheet with a nonstick baking mat or parchment paper.

3. In a medium bowl, whisk together the coconut flour and baking powder.

4. Melt the cheese in a large microwave-safe bowl, on high, for 30 seconds or until it is melted.

5. Add the flour mixture and the eggs to the melted cheese and knead the dough using a rubber spatula or your hands. Knead the dough into a ball and then divide into 8 equal pieces.

6. Roll each portion out into a log about 8 inches (20 cm) long and pinch the ends of the log together to form a bagel.

7. If you're adding a bagel topping, place it on a plate and press each bagel onto the topping so some of it sticks to the top. Alternatively, you can brush each bagel with some melted butter or egg wash and sprinkle the topping over each bagel.

8. Place the bagels on the baking sheet spaced 2 inches (5 cm) apart and bake for 15 to 20 minutes, or until the bagels are lightly browned.

9. Cool. Store in the refrigerator for a few days or freeze for a few months.

YIELD: 8 bagels

PER SERVING: 169 calories; 6 g carbohydrate; 11 g fat; 13 g protein; 3 g fiber

PUMPKIN BREAD

∙DAIRY-FREE ∙GRAIN-FREE ∙GLUTEN-FREE

This pumpkin bread boasts an array of spices, including nutmeg, ginger, cinnamon, and cloves, that have natural anti-inflammatory properties.

I use a 7.5×3.5×2.25-inch (19×9×6 cm) loaf pan, but you can use a slightly larger pan for a lower profile loaf. This is not a heavy bread, so a thin layer of either the Maple Cream Cheese Frosting (page 100) or the Maple Cream Frosting (page 101) goes well on the top of the bread, once it has cooled.

I recommend a low-carb sweetener with bulk however, if you'd like to use stevia, use 20 drops of liquid stevia or 1 teaspoon powdered stevia.

½ cup (120 g) roasted butternut squash purée (see page 62) or pumpkin purée, canned or freshly roasted

½ cup low-carb 1:1 sweetener, or equivalent (see chart on page 15)

4 large eggs

¼ teaspoon baking soda

¼ teaspoon salt

½ teaspoon ground nutmeg

½ teaspoon ground cinnamon

½ teaspoon ground cloves

½ teaspoon ground ginger

¼ cup plus 2 tablespoons (39 g) coconut flour

1. Preheat your oven to 350°F (180°C, or gas mark 4).

2. Prepare a baking pan by greasing it generously or lining the bottom with parchment paper and greasing the sides.

3. Add the squash, sweetener, and eggs to a medium-size bowl and blend well.

4. Add the baking soda, salt, nutmeg, cinnamon, cloves, ginger, and coconut flour to the wet mixture and use a handheld or stand mixer to blend well. Let the batter sit for few minutes and mix once more.

5. Transfer the batter to the baking pan and bake for 40 minutes, or until a toothpick inserted in the center comes out clean.

6. Cool and frost. Store in a sealed container at room temperature for a few days, in the refrigerator for a few weeks, or in the freezer for a few months.

YIELD: 1 loaf, or 10 servings

PER SERVING: 52 calories; 5 g carbohydrate; 3 g fat; 3 g protein; 2 g fiber

CINNAMON RAISIN BREAD

•EGG-FREE   •DAIRY-FREE   •NUT-FREE OPTION   •GRAIN-FREE   •GLUTEN-FREE

This is a great everyday bread, slightly sweeter than sandwich bread, using both almond butter and almond flour. You can use either raw or roasted almond butter, but be sure to use the creamy version unless you want nut pieces in your bread. The higher carb count is from the raisins, so if you'd prefer a lower carb count, remove the raisins or reduce the amount. To make this nut-free, use sunflower butter instead of almond butter and ground sunflower seeds in place of almond flour.

Note: The raisins tend to sink through the bread while baking, so I recommend chopping the raisins into smaller pieces and adding half of them to the top of the bread before you place the loaf in the oven to bake.

¾ cup (190 g) smooth almond butter

4 eggs

2 tablespoons low-carb 1:1 sweetener, or equivalent (see chart on page 15)

¼ cup (24 g) blanched almond flour

½ teaspoon salt

½ teaspoon baking soda

1 teaspoon ground cinnamon

½ cup (72 g) raisins, chopped

1. Preheat your oven to 350°F (175°C, or gas mark 4).

2. Line a loaf pan with parchment paper. I either line the entire pan or line the bottom and then grease the sides. I use a smaller pan, about 4×7 inches (10×17.8 cm), but any pan around this size will work.

3. Using a spatula or mixer, blend the almond butter, eggs, and sweetener in a large bowl until creamy.

4. In another bowl, blend the almond flour, salt, baking soda, and cinnamon together.

5. Add the dry mixture to the almond butter batter and blend well.

6. Stir half the raisins into the batter and pour the batter into the baking pan. Sprinkle the rest of the raisins on top.

7. Bake for 45 minutes, or until a long toothpick or wood skewer inserted into the center comes out clean. Make sure the bottom of the loaf is baked as well.

8. Cool and slice. Store sealed in the refrigerator for a week or so, or in the freezer for a few months.

YIELD: 1 loaf, or 8 servings

PER SERVING: 266 calories; 27 g carbohydrate; 16 g fat; 9 g protein; 4 g fiber

CHAPTER 3

WAFFLES, PANCAKES, MUFFINS, AND DONUTS

From savory Mushroom–Feta Spinach Crêpes (page 76) to Vanilla Donuts (page 69), this chapter showcases an array of snack and meal ideas. While you might certainly think of crêpes, muffins, and donuts as breakfast treats, these recipes make great everyday snacks since they're loaded with protein, good fat, and fiber.

SAVORY WAFFLES

·NUT-FREE   ·GRAIN-FREE   ·GLUTEN-FREE

These savory waffles make a great base for a meal. Add some grilled chicken or chopped ham or bacon, sliced avocados, a few diced tomatoes, and salad dressing and you have a meal. Or try adding a fried egg and some salsa. For the pepper Jack cheese, feel free to substitute Monterey Jack or other savory cheese. If you use a mellow cheese, you might want to add a bit more salt or maybe a dash of hot sauce to the batter.

4 large eggs

1 teaspoon olive oil or other oil

½ cup (56 g) trimmed and finely sliced scallions (about 3 onions)

¾ cup (80 g) grated pepper Jack cheese or other cheese

¼ teaspoon baking soda

Pinch salt (less than ⅛ teaspoon)

2 tablespoons (13 g) coconut flour

1. Preheat your waffle iron to a medium heat.

2. Mix all the ingredients together using a mixer or whisk. Let the batter sit for a few minutes and mix once more.

3. Scoop ½ cup to 1 cup (120 to 235 ml) batter, depending on the size of your waffle iron, and pour onto the iron. Cook the waffle on medium heat, following the manufacturer's directions.

4. Serve warm. The waffles can be stored in a sealed container in the refrigerator for about a week or in the freezer for a few months.

YIELD: 4 large waffles

PER SERVING: 183 calories; 4 g carbohydrate; 13 g fat; 12 g protein; 2 g fiber

FLUFFY PANCAKES

•DAIRY-FREE OPTION   •GRAIN-FREE   •GLUTEN-FREE

This is a great combination of almond and coconut flour that results in thick pancakes. The yogurt enhances the rise, or fluffiness. You can make these larger if you'd like just cook them a bit longer on the first side, before flipping.

If you'd like to make this dairy-free, I recommend using dairy-free yogurt because yogurt is acidic. The trick to getting thick, fluffy pancakes is to add something acidic to the batter to react with the baking soda. The reaction of baking soda and yogurt creates carbon dioxide gas bubbles, which help the pancakes rise.

¼ cup (26 g) coconut flour

1 cup (96 g) almond flour

½ teaspoon baking soda

3 eggs

¼ cup (62 g) yogurt

½ cup (120 ml) water

2 tablespoons low-carb 1:1 sweetener, or equivalent (see chart on page 15)

½ teaspoon vanilla extract

1 tablespoon (15 ml) oil, plus more for the skillet

Pinch salt (about ⅛ teaspoon)

1. Add all the ingredients to a food processor or blender and pulse for 10 seconds or so to combine. Alternatively, combine all the dry ingredients in a large bowl, then add the wet ingredients and mix well.

2. Preheat your skillet over low to medium heat.

3. Add 1 to 2 tablespoons (15 to 30 ml) of cooking oil to the skillet and heat until just shimmering.

4. Spoon 1½ tablespoons (23 ml) of batter for each pancake into the skillet.

5. Cook the pancakes well on the first side, for about a few minutes. Bubbles may start to appear on the top of each pancake. Once the pancake is starting to brown around the edges and bottom, flip it to the other side and cook for another minute or so.

6. Place the pancakes on a plate and continue until you've used up all the batter.

7. Store leftover pancakes in the refrigerator for a few days, or freeze for a few months.

YIELD: 12 small pancakes

PER SERVING: 62 calories; 4 g carbohydrate; 4 g fat; 3 g protein; 1 g fiber

CHOCOLATE CHIP SCONES
WITH ALMOND FLOUR

•DAIRY-FREE OPTION   •GRAIN-FREE   •GLUTEN-FREE

Scones are a great treat any time of day, and they pack well for travel. If you'd like these scones a bit moister, add 1 tablespoon (15 ml) of cream, milk, or yogurt in step 2.

To make them dairy-free, you can use dairy-free milk, such as almond or coconut milk, or dairy-free yogurt works as well.

2 cups (192 g) blanched almond flour

1 teaspoon baking soda

¼ teaspoon sea salt

1 large egg

2 tablespoons low-carb 1:1 sweetener, or equivalent (see chart on page 15)

2 tablespoons (30 ml) milk, cream, or yogurt

½ cup (84 g) sugar-free chocolate chips

1. Preheat your oven to 350°F (180°C, or gas mark 4).

2. In a bowl, add the almond flour, baking soda, and salt and blend with a spatula or spoon. Then add the egg, sweetener, milk, and chocolate chips. Blend well. The dough will be thick.

3. Pat the dough into a ball and place it on parchment paper or a nonstick surface.

4. With a rolling pin, roll the dough into a large circle, or two circles, and slice it into 8 triangular pieces. Use a cold knife to slice the scones.

5. Place the scones and parchment paper (or nonstick mat) on a baking sheet and separate the scones so they're about 1 inch (2.5 cm) or so apart.

6. Bake for 7 to 10 minutes, or until the scones are lightly browned.

7. Cool the scones. Store in a sealed container or the refrigerator.

YIELD: 8 scones

PER SERVING: 213 calories; 10 g carbohydrate; 18 g fat; 8 g protein; 5 g fiber

ENGLISH MUFFINS

‧DAIRY-FREE ‧GRAIN-FREE ‧GLUTEN-FREE

This is a quick and easy recipe, especially when you're craving an English muffin.

You can stretch this recipe to get four thin slices, but most of the time you'll get two thick slices or three thinner slices.

I recommend a 3½-inch (9-cm) ramekin, which holds about 4 ounces (120 ml) of liquid. A slightly larger diameter will work as well, and yield closer to two slices.

If you don't have a microwave or don't use one, you can bake the muffin, but it does crumble a bit. To bake it, generously oil the inside of the ramekin or bowl, and bake in a preheated oven or toaster oven at 400°F (200°C, or gas mark 6) for 15 minutes, or until solid. You may need to slide a knife along the sides to wiggle the muffin out of the ramekin.

¼ cup (24 g) blanched almond flour

1 tablespoon (6.5 g) coconut flour

⅛ teaspoon baking soda

⅛ teaspoon salt

1 large egg white

½ teaspoon oil

2 tablespoons (30 ml) warm water

1. Add the flours, baking soda, and salt to a small ramekin or microwave-safe bowl, and mix well with a fork.

2. Add the egg white, oil, and water, and mix well.

3. With a fork, spoon, or your fingers, flatten the batter so it's even on top.

4. Microwave the ramekin for 2 minutes.

5. Turn the ramekin upside down to slide out the muffin.

6. Slice in into 2 muffin halves and toast each slice.

7. Spread with butter, peanut butter, jam, or scrambled egg.

YIELD: 2 muffin halves

PER SERVING: 114 calories; 5 g carbohydrate; 1 g fat; 5 g protein; 3 g fiber

CHOCOLATE CHIP SCONES
WITH COCONUT FLOUR

·DAIRY-FREE OPTION   ·NUT-FREE   ·GRAIN-FREE   ·GLUTEN-FREE

Scones pair well with your relaxing morning cup of tea or coffee, but they are also a great on-the-run breakfast meal or snack. These chocolate chip scones are a bit on the lighter side, as far as scones go, thanks to the lightness of coconut flour. This recipe makes a good number of scones, so stash some away in the freezer for a later date.

To make these dairy-free, for the yogurt substitute coconut milk or other dairy-free yogurt or coconut cream.

4 large eggs

¼ cup (57 g) unsalted butter, melted, coconut oil, or ghee

¾ cup (173 g) plain yogurt, crème frâiche, or sour cream

¼ cup low-carb 1:1 sweetener, or equivalent (see chart on page 15)

½ teaspoon salt

½ teaspoon baking soda

¾ cup (78 g) coconut flour

½ cup (84 g) chocolate chips

1. Preheat your oven to 350°F (180°C, or gas mark 4).

2. Generously grease a baking sheet, or line it with parchment paper or nonstick mat.

3. Add the eggs, butter, yogurt, sweetener, salt, and baking soda to a bowl and mix, using a handheld or stand mixer, until well blended.

4. Add the coconut flour to the batter and mix until well blended. Stir in the chocolate chips. Let the batter sit for a few minutes and mix again. The batter should be mushy and easy to spoon and drop onto the baking sheet. If you find it's still too stiff, you can add another tablespoon of coconut milk or water.

5. For each scone, spoon between 1 to 2 tablespoons (about 42 g) of batter onto the baking sheet and shape it a bit with your fingers or a spoon.

6. Bake for 25 minutes or until the biscuits are browning on the bottom and edges and are a bit tender to touch.

7. Cool and serve warm or at room temperature. Store in a sealed container at room temperature for a few days or in the freezer for a few months.

YIELD: 16 scones

PER SERVING: 113 calories; 10 g carbohydrate; 7 g fat; 3 g protein; 3 g fiber

SILVER DOLLAR PANCAKES

•GLUTEN-FREE •GRAIN-FREE •DAIRY-FREE •LOW-SUGAR •NUT-FREE

Make these pancakes the size of silver dollars (on the small side) by dropping about a tablespoon of batter on a skillet for each one. You can make them larger by using about 2 tablespoons (about 22 g) and pouring it around or tilting the pan around in a circle to spread the batter. If you're finding your pancakes taste a bit too much like an omelet ("too eggy"), try adding about ½ to 1 tablespoon (4 to 7 g) more coconut flour. This can make the difference for some folks.

3 large eggs

1 teaspoon high-heat cooking oil, ghee, or coconut oil, plus more for cooking

½ teaspoon vanilla extract

1 teaspoon low-carb 1:1 sweetener; or equivalent (see chart on page 15)

¼ teaspoon ground cinnamon (optional)

¼ teaspoon baking soda

⅛ teaspoon salt

2 tablespoons (13 g) coconut flour

1. Whisk together the eggs, 1 teaspoon oil, the vanilla, and the honey.

2. Add the cinnamon, baking soda, salt, and coconut flour to the wet ingredients, and whisk until well blended. Let the batter sit for a few minutes so the coconut flour can absorb the moisture, then whisk again to remove any remaining lumps.

3. Preheat a skillet on low to medium heat. Add a generous amount of cooking oil to coat the entire skillet.

4. Pour about 1 tablespoon (11 g) of batter for each pancake in the skillet without letting the edges of the pancakes touch. Let the pancakes cook slowly to avoid burning the bottoms. Flip the pancakes after a few minutes or when the edges begin to brown and you can easily slide a spatula under the pancake. They will take a bit longer to cook on each side than the average pancake. Repeat for the remaining batter, adding more cooking oil as necessary. Serve warm.

YIELD: About 12 silver dollar-size pancakes, or about 3 servings

PER SERVING: 50 calories; 2 g carbohydrate; 4 g fat; 2 g protein; 1 g fiber

CINNAMON BUN MUFFINS

•DAIRY-FREE OPTION •GRAIN-FREE •GLUTEN-FREE

This is a popular recipe on my site, and for good reason. The flavor of cinnamon and butter and the lightness of the coconut flour batter make it a tender sweet muffin without all the carbs. You can use any low-carb sweetener you prefer. Recipe testers have had great success using stevia as well as bulk sweeteners. To use stevia, add ½ teaspoon to the muffin batter and ¼ teaspoon to the topping.

To make this dairy-free, replace the butter with coconut oil.

FOR MUFFINS:

½ cup (52 g) coconut flour

¼ teaspoon baking soda

¼ teaspoon salt

4 eggs

⅓ cup (80 ml) coconut milk or other milk

½ cup low-carb 1:1 sweetener, or equivalent (see chart on page 15)

FOR CINNAMON TOPPING:

2 tablespoons (12 g) ground cinnamon

2 tablespoons (28 g) unsalted butter, melted

4 tablespoons (¼ cup) low-carb 1:1 sweetener, or equivalent (see chart on page 15)

¼ cup (35 g) chopped walnuts (optional)

1. Preheat your oven to 350°F (175°C, or gas mark 4).

2. Prepare 8 cups of a muffin pan with nonstick liners.

3. To make the muffins: Combine the coconut flour, baking soda, and salt in a large bowl and blend well.

4. Add the eggs, milk, and sweetener to the dry mixture and blend well by hand or in a food processor or high-speed blender.

5. To make the topping: Combine all the ingredients in a bowl and whisk to blend well.

6. Fill each muffin liner about ¼ of the way with batter.

7. Sprinkle ½ to 1 tablespoon (7 to 14 g) of topping over each muffin and then fill with the remaining batter.

8. Sprinkle the remaining topping over each muffin and use a toothpick or fork to blend the topping in just a bit.

9. Bake for 24 minutes, or until a toothpick inserted into the center of a muffin comes out clean.

10. Cool. Store in the refrigerator for a few weeks, or freeze for a few months.

YIELD: 8 muffins

PER SERVING: 122 calories; 7 g carbohydrate; 9 g fat; 5 g protein; 4 g fiber

PUMPKIN MUFFINS

∙DAIRY-FREE   ∙GRAIN-FREE   ∙GLUTEN-FREE

Here's a simple pumpkin muffin that can be made as regular-size muffins or mini-muffins. Like many muffin recipes using coconut flour, this one is light and works well with a variety of spices and sweeteners. You can use canned pumpkin here, or freshly roasted squash. My favorite squash purée is roasted butternut squash (see below).

½ cup (120 g) butternut squash or pumpkin purée

½ cup low-carb 1:1 sweetener, or equivalent (see chart on page 15)

4 large eggs

¼ teaspoon baking soda

¼ teaspoon salt

½ teaspoon ground nutmeg

½ teaspoon ground cinnamon

½ teaspoon ground cloves

½ teaspoon ground ginger

¼ cup plus 2 tablespoons (39 g) coconut flour

1. Preheat your oven to 350°F (180°C, or gas mark 4).

2. Prepare a muffin pan by lining the muffin wells with liners. Grease the liners unless they are nonstick liners.

3. Place the purée, sweetener, and eggs in a bowl and blend well. I use a mixer for this batter.

4. Add the baking soda, salt, nutmeg, cinnamon, cloves, and ginger to the wet ingredients and mix well. Let the batter sit for a few minutes and then mix again.

5. Fill the muffin liners two-thirds full and bake for 15 minutes, or until a toothpick inserted in the center of a muffin comes out clean.

6. Cool and serve. Store in a sealed container at room temperature for a few days, in the refrigerator for a few weeks, or in the freezer for a few months.

YIELD: 8 muffins

PER SERVING: 66 calories; 6 g carbohydrate; 3 g fat; 4 g protein; 2 g fiber

HOW TO ROAST BUTTERNUT SQUASH

Here's a simple method for making roasted squash that can be used for muffins and pies calling for pumpkin or squash purée, or in recipes calling for diced roasted squash.

Preheat your oven to 400°F (200°C, or gas mark 6). Slice one butternut squash in half lengthwise, and then scoop out the seeds. Rub the inside of each squash half with coconut oil, ghee, or other high-heat oil, and place on a greased or parchment-lined baking sheet, cut side up. Roast for about 30 minutes or until the squash is tender and you can insert a fork in the thickest part.

Cool, and then cut into cubes for recipes needing diced cooked squash. To make purée, scoop out the squash and purée it in a blender. If it's dry you may need to add a bit of water. Leftover squash may be kept in a sealed container in the refrigerator for a few days or in the freezer for a few months.

WAFFLES

·DAIRY-FREE   ·NUT-FREE OPTION   ·GRAIN-FREE   ·GLUTEN-FREE

Here's a simple and reliable recipe for waffles that calls for almond flour, but feel free to use any nut or seed flour you like. Pecan waffles are a bit darker and have a rich flavor. Cashew waffles, using cashew flour, are slightly lighter in color and texture.

For more of a multigrain texture, use almond meal instead of almond flour. For nut-free waffles, replace the almond flour with finely ground sunflower seeds or pumpkin seeds.

1 cup (96 g) almond flour

¼ teaspoon salt

4 eggs

1 teaspoon vanilla extract

2 tablespoons low-carb 1:1 sweetener, or equivalent (see chart on page 15)

1. Warm up your waffle iron.

2. Place the dry ingredients in a mixing bowl, and blend well with a whisk.

3. Add the wet ingredients to the dry ingredients and whisk until well blended.

4. Follow the directions on how much batter to add to your waffle iron and then close the lid.

5. When the waffle is ready, take it out and place it on a warm plate. Continue until all the batter is used.

6. Store the waffles sealed in the refrigerator for a week or so, or freeze for a few months.

YIELD: 6 waffles

PER SERVING: 76 calories; 2 g carbohydrate; 6 g fat; 5 g protein; 1 g fiber

SANDWICH ROLLS

·DAIRY-FREE OPTION   ·GRAIN-FREE   ·GLUTEN-FREE

I recommend using a nonstick muffin top baking pan, but you can use a donut pan to make bagels or muffin rings (see reources page 154).

To make this dairy-free replace the butter will coconut oil.

1 cup (96 g) almond flour

¼ teaspoon baking soda

¼ teaspoon salt

4 tablespoons (56 g) unsalted butter, melted

4 large eggs

2 tablespoons (30 ml) almond milk (or other milk)

2 tablespoons (12 g) bagel topping (poppy seeds, sesame seeds, salt, or other topping)

1. Preheat your oven to 425°F (220°C, or gas mark 7).

2. Combine the almond flour, baking soda, and salt in a mixer bowl or other bowl and mix to blend.

3. Add the wet ingredients to the bowl and mix to blend well.

4. Divide the batter among 6 muffin ring molds or a muffin top baking pan (nonstick), shuffle the pan to even out the dough, and bake for 12 to 14 minutes or until the rolls begin to turn golden brown.

5. Cool. Store sealed in the refrigerator for several days.

YIELD: 6 servings (3 rolls)

PER SERVING: 143 calories; 1 g carbohydrate; 13 g fat; 5 g protein; 1 g fiber

CHOCOLATE CHIP MUFFINS

·DAIRY-FREE OPTION   ·NUT-FREE   ·GRAIN-FREE   ·GLUTEN-FREE

I enjoy chocolate added to just about any treat, and of course chocolate is a treat itself. So here are simple muffins with chocolate chips. They're really more like cakes or cupcakes, but that won't stop you from eating them any time of day.

To make these dairy-free, substitute coconut oil or olive oil for the butter.

½ cup (52 g) coconut flour

¼ teaspoon baking soda

¼ teaspoon salt

4 large eggs

⅓ cup (76 g) unsalted butter, melted

½ cup low-carb 1:1 sweetener, or equivalent (see chart on page 15)

1 tablespoon (15 ml) vanilla extract

2 tablespoons (28 ml) coconut milk or other milk

⅓ cup (56 g) sugar-free chocolate chips

1. Preheat your oven to 350°F (180°C, or gas mark 4).

2. Add the coconut flour, baking soda, and salt to a large bowl and blend well.

3. Add the eggs, butter, honey, vanilla, and coconut milk to the dry ingredients and use a handheld or stand mixer to blend well. Gently stir in the chocolate chips, using a spoon or spatula.

4. Line muffin tins and fill about three-quarters of the way with batter. Bake for 20 minutes, or until a toothpick inserted in the center of a cupcake comes out clean.

5. Cool and frost. Store the cupcakes, covered, at room temperature for a few days, in the refrigerator for a few weeks, or in the freezer for a few months.

YIELD: 8 muffins

PER SERVING: 168 calories; 16 g carbohydrate; 13 g fat; 5 g protein; 3 g fiber

CHOCOLATE DONUTS

•DAIRY-FREE OPTION   •NUT-FREE   •GRAIN-FREE   •GLUTEN-FREE

I favor the old-fashioned cake style of donut. I usually make these in a regular-size donut pan that bakes in the oven, but you can also use an electric donut maker or mini-donut maker to whip up a batch of these delightful treats.

To make these dairy-free, use coconut oil in place of butter.

½ cup (52 g) coconut flour

¼ teaspoon salt

¼ teaspoon baking soda

¼ cup (20 g) unsweetened cocoa powder

6 large eggs

½ cup low-carb 1:1 sweetener, or equivalent (see chart on page 15)

1 tablespoon (15 ml) vanilla extract

½ cup plus 1 tablespoon (126 g) unsalted butter, melted

1. Preheat your oven to 350°F (180°C, or gas mark 4).

2. Generously grease the donut pan or follow the instructions for your donut maker.

3. Blend the flour, salt, baking soda, and cocoa together in a bowl.

4. Add the eggs, sweetener, vanilla, and butter to the dry ingredients and mix using a handheld or stand mixer. Let the batter sit for a few minutes and mix once more.

5. Fill the donut pan wells about two-thirds of the way with batter.

6. Bake for 20 minutes, or until a toothpick inserted in the center of a donut comes out clean.

7. Cool and serve. Store in a sealed container for a few days at room temperature, in the refrigerator for a few weeks, or in the freezer for a few months.

YIELD: 8 donuts

PER SERVING: 209 calories; 17 g carbohydrate; 18 g fat; 6 g protein; 3 g fiber

VANILLA DONUTS

·GLUTEN-FREE   ·GRAIN-FREE   ·DAIRY-FREE OPTION   ·NUT-FREE

Here's a versatile vanilla donut that you can have plain or frost.

This recipe works with any kind or size of donut pan, including a donut pan for your oven, an electric donut maker, and a mini-donut maker.

To make this dairy-free use either coconut oil in place of butter.

½ cup (52 g) coconut flour

½ teaspoon baking soda

¼ teaspoon salt

¼ teaspoon ground cinnamon

4 large eggs

¼ cup (57 g) unsalted butter, melted

¼ cup (60 ml) coconut milk or other milk

¼ cup low-carb 1:1 sweetener, or equivalent (see chart on page 15)

1 tablespoon (15 ml) vanilla extract

1 teaspoon lemon juice

1. Preheat your oven to 350°F (180°C, or gas mark 4).

2. Grease your donut pan or follow the directions for your donut maker.

3. Place the coconut flour, baking soda, and salt in a bowl and blend well.

4. Add the eggs, butter, milk, sweetener, and vanilla to a separate mixing bowl and blend well.

5. Add the dry mix to the wet mix and blend well using a handheld or stand mixer. Let the batter stand for a few minutes and mix once more.

6. Fill the donut pan or maker with batter so it reaches the top of the donut well. To make it easy to fill the donut pan, place the batter in a resealable plastic bag, cut a small piece from one corner, and pipe the batter into the donut wells.

7. For regular-size donuts, bake for 15 minutes, or until a toothpick inserted in the center of the donut comes out clean. If you're using an electric donut maker, follow the manufacturer's directions. My mini-donut maker bakes these donuts in about 3 minutes.

8. Cool the donuts.

YIELD: 8 donuts

PER SERVING: 126 calories; 17 g carbohydrate; 6 g fat; 4 g protein; 3 g fiber

CINNAMON DONUTS

•NUT-FREE   •DAIRY-FREE OPTION   •GRAIN-FREE   •GLUTEN-FREE

Cinnamon coating on vanilla donuts is an easy donut topping option or a replacement for glazing or frosting your donut. To make this dairy-free, use coconut oil instead of butter or ghee.

FOR DONUTS:

½ cup (52 g) coconut flour

½ teaspoon baking soda

¼ teaspoon salt

¼ teaspoon ground cinnamon

4 large eggs

¼ cup (57 g) unsalted butter, melted, or ghee

¼ cup (60 ml) coconut milk or other milk

¼ cup low-carb 1:1 sweetener, or equivalent (see chart on page 15)

1 tablespoon (15 ml) vanilla extract

1 teaspoon lemon juice

FOR CINNAMON-SUGAR TOPPING:

¼ cup low-carb 1:1 sweetener, or equivalent (see chart on page 15)

2 tablespoons (14 g) ground cinnamon

¼ cup (57 g) unsalted butter, melted

1. Preheat your oven to 350°F (180°C, or gas mark 4) and grease your donut pan or follow the directions for your donut maker.

2. **To make the donuts:** Place the coconut flour, baking soda, salt, and cinnamon in a bowl and blend well.

3. Add the eggs, butter, milk, sweetener, and vanilla to a mixing bowl and blend well.

4. Add the dry mix to the wet mix and blend well using a handheld or stand mixer. Let the batter stand for a few minutes and mix once more.

5. Fill the donut pan or maker with batter so it reaches the top of the donut well. To make it easy to fill the donut pan, place the batter in a resealable plastic bag, cut a small piece from one corner, and pipe in the batter.

6. Bake the donuts for 15 minutes for regular-size donuts, or until a toothpick inserted in the center of the donut comes out clean. If you're using an electric donut maker, follow the manufacturer's directions. My mini-donut maker bakes these donuts in about 3 minutes.

7. Cool the donuts before dipping them in the topping.

8. **To make the topping:** Mix the sweetener and cinnamon together and place the mixture on a plate. Melt the butter and place in a bowl or on a plate.

9. Dip the top of each donut in the butter and then in the cinnamon sugar mixture.

YIELD: 8 donuts

PER SERVING (WITHOUT TOPPING): 126 calories; 17 g carbohydrate; 9 g fat; 4 g protein; 3 g fiber

COCONUT FLOUR DONUTS

·DAIRY-FREE OPTION   ·NUT-FREE   ·GRAIN-FREE   ·GLUTEN-FREE

Chocolate makes a great topping for this cake-like donut. These are a bit denser than the Vanilla Donuts, and they were one of the first coconut flour recipes that I created, way back when I started *Comfy Belly*.

You can dress these up in a number of ways or just eat them straight up. Or make them as cupcakes, cool, and top with Chocolate Frosting on page 98.

To make these dairy-free, replace the butter with coconut oil.

½ cup (52 g) coconut flour

¼ teaspoon salt

¼ teaspoon baking soda

6 large eggs

½ cup low-carb 1:1 sweetener, or equivalent (see chart on page 15)

1 tablespoon (15 ml) vanilla extract

½ cup (114 g) unsalted butter, melted

1. Preheat your oven to 350°F (180°C, or gas mark 4).

2. Grease your donut pan or follow the directions for your donut maker.

3. In a bowl, whisk together the coconut flour, salt, and baking soda.

4. In a separate bowl, add the eggs, sweetener, vanilla, and butter and blend together, using a handheld or stand mixer.

5. Add the dry ingredients to the wet ingredients and blend well. Let the batter sit for a few minutes and mix again.

6. Fill the donut wells two-thirds of the way. Follow manufacturer's instructions if you're using a donut maker.

7. Bake the donuts for 15 minutes, or until a toothpick inserted in the center comes out clean.

8. Let the donuts cool. Store in a sealed container at room temperature for a few days, in the refrigerator for a few weeks, or in the freezer for a few months.

YIELD: 8 donuts

PER SERVING: 190 calories; 16 g carbohydrate; 16 g fat; 6 g protein; 3 g fiber

CRÊPES

•DAIRY-FREE OPTION   •NUT-FREE   •GRAIN-FREE   •GLUTEN-FREE

A crêpe is a light, thin pancake that is filled with a few sweet or savory ingredients. Some popular sweet fillings include jam, fruit, nut butter, and chocolate. For savory fillings, just think of your favorite stir-fry mixture or any other savory filling that likes a bit of a wrapping around it.

If you're using this crêpe recipe with a savory filling, omit the honey and add some pepper or other spices that go well with your filling. For a sweet crêpe filling, see Berry Yogurt Crêpes (page 75). For a savory crêpe filling, see the Mushroom-Feta Spinach Crêpes (page 76).

To make this dairy-free, replace the butter with coconut oil.

FOR SWEET CRÊPES:

2 large eggs

2 tablespoons (28 g) unsalted butter, melted, plus more for the skillet

1 teaspoon low-carb 1:1 sweetener, or equivalent (see chart on page 15)

⅓ cup (80 ml) coconut milk or other milk

2 tablespoons (13 g) coconut flour

⅛ teaspoon salt

FOR SAVORY CRÊPES:

2 eggs

2 tablespoons (28 g) unsalted butter, melted, plus more for the skillet

⅓ cup (80ml) coconut milk or other milk

2 tablespoons (13 g) coconut flour

⅛ teaspoon salt

1. Whisk together the eggs, 2 tablespoons (28 g) butter, sweetener (omit for savory crêpes), and milk.

2. Add the coconut flour and salt and whisk until well blended. Let the batter sit for a few minutes and mix once more.

3. Warm a skillet over medium heat and add about 1 tablespoon (15 ml) oil. Pour about 2 tablespoons (about 22 g) batter into the skillet to make a 4-to-5-inch (10-to-13-cm) crêpe. Tilt the pan to allow the batter to spread across skillet in the shape of a circle.

4. Cook for a few minutes, until the edges and bottom are starting to brown and you can easily slip a spatula underneath; flip the crêpe over. Cook another minute or so, or until it is slightly browned.

5. Transfer the cooked crêpe onto a plate and repeat with the rest of the batter. Place wax paper, parchment paper, or paper towels between the crêpes on the plate to keep them from sticking together.

6. Serve warm. Store in a sealed container in the refrigerator for a week or in the freezer for a month.

YIELD: 6 crêpes

PER SERVING: 46 calories; 1 g carbohydrate; 4 g fat; 0 g protein; 9 g fiber

BERRY YOGURT CRÊPES

•DAIRY-FREE OPTION   •NUT-FREE   •GRAIN-FREE   •GLUTEN-FREE

Here's a quick recipe for adding simmered berries and yogurt to sweet crêpes. Of course you can add fresh berries as well, but I favor the simmered berries because they are almost like a fresh jam. In a pinch you can use jam and yogurt.

To make this dairy-free, use dairy-free yogurt and make the dairy-free version of the sweet crêpes by replacing the butter with coconut oil.

4 Sweet Crêpes (page 73)

1 cup (230 g) yogurt

1 recipe Berry Filling (recipe follows)

1. Lay the crêpes flat and place about ¼ cup (60 g) yogurt and ¼ cup berry filling on the center of each crêpe.

2. Fold each crêpe closed.

3. Serve warm or at room temperature.

YIELD: 4 crêpes

PER SERVING: 73 calories; 15 g carbohydrate; 4 g fat; 0 g protein; 9 g fiber

BERRY FILLING

A little simmering and you have a sweet little pot of berries you can add to yogurt or ice cream, or freeze for later.

1 cup (150 g) fresh blueberries, raspberries, blackberries, or other berries

1 tablespoon (15 ml) lemon juice

2 tablespoons low-carb 1:1 sweetener, or equivalent (see chart on page 15)

Pinch salt (less than ⅛ teaspoon)

1. Add all the ingredients to a saucepan and simmer for 10 minutes, stirring occasionally.

2. Cool and serve. Store in the refrigerator for a week or in the freezer for a few months.

YIELD: 1 cup (120 g)

MUSHROOM-FETA SPINACH CRÊPES

·GRAIN-FREE   ·GLUTEN-FREE

Skillet scrambles and quick stir-fried mixes go well in crêpes. You can make the crêpes ahead of time and store them sealed in the refrigerator until you're ready to whip up a scramble. Here's one of my favorite skillet scrambles that makes a great meal. Serve it with Pico de Gallo (page 142) or Roasted Cherry Tomatoes (page 153).

2 tablespoons (30 ml) ghee, coconut oil, or other oil

½ cup (30 g) chopped cremini or other mushrooms

5 ounces (142 g) fresh spinach leaves, chopped

½ cup (50 g) chopped scallions

4½ ounces (127 g) feta cheese

1 large egg

4 Savory Crêpes (page 73)

1. Warm a skillet on medium-high heat and add the ghee. Add the mushrooms to the skillet and cook, stirring occasionally, for 5 minutes, or until they begin to soften and brown.

2. Lower the heat to medium and add the spinach and onions. Cook for 5 minutes, stirring occasionally.

3. Turn off the heat and add the egg. Blend well.

4. Fill each crêpe with some scramble and serve warm.

YIELD: 4 servings

PER SERVING: 479 calories; 12 g carbohydrate; 39 g fat; 23 g protein; 11 g fiber

CHAPTER 4

CAKES AND CUPCAKES

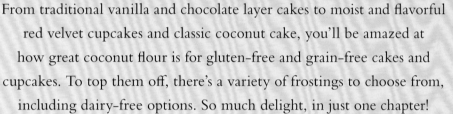

From traditional vanilla and chocolate layer cakes to moist and flavorful red velvet cupcakes and classic coconut cake, you'll be amazed at how great coconut flour is for gluten-free and grain-free cakes and cupcakes. To top them off, there's a variety of frostings to choose from, including dairy-free options. So much delight, in just one chapter!

YELLOW CAKE

‣DAIRY-FREE OPTION ‣GRAIN-FREE ‣GLUTEN-FREE

Almond and coconut flours are combined in this simple layer cake to give you the best of both worlds. A light, spongy cake that soaks up sweetness around it, it's a nice alternative to yellow cake made with just almond flour. This cake works well as a celebratory cake with frosting or other toppings.

This recipe is for a single cake layer, baked in an 8-inch (20-cm) round pan. To make a two-layer cake, double the recipe and split the batter between two 8-inch (20-cm) cake pans.

To make this dairy-free, use coconut oil in place of butter or ghee, or use another oil such as olive oil.

½ cup (48 g) blanched almond flour

¼ cup (26 g) coconut flour

¼ teaspoon salt

¼ teaspoon baking soda

3 eggs

¼ cup (56 g) unsalted butter or ghee, melted

3 tablespoons low-carb 1:1 sweetener, or equivalent (see chart on page 15)

½ cup (120 ml) almond milk (or other dairy-free milk)

1 teaspoon vanilla extract

1. Preheat your oven to 325°F (170°C, or gas mark 3).

2. Line the bottom of an 8-inch (20-cm) round cake pan with a parchment paper circle or other nonstick covering, or grease the pan well.

3. Blend the almond and coconut flours, salt, and baking soda in a mixing bowl. Add all the wet ingredients and blend well.

4. Pour the batter into the prepared pan and bake for 20 minutes, or until a toothpick inserted into the center of the cake comes out clean.

5. Let the cake cool on a wire rack for about 15 minutes, or an hour if you plan to frost the cake. Gently run a knife around the outside edge of the cake to make it easy to remove.

6. Once completely cooled, store covered at room temperature for a week or so, or store in the refrigerator for a few weeks.

YIELD: 1 cake layer (8 servings) or 8 cupcakes

PER SERVING: 147 calories; 5 g carbohydrate; 13 g fat; 4 g protein; 2 g fiber

CHOCOLATE CUPCAKES

·DAIRY-FREE   ·GRAIN-FREE   ·GLUTEN-FREE

This recipe creates a tender chocolate cupcake that can be eaten as is or frosted. I recommend the Vanilla Buttercream Frosting (page 99) or the Chocolate Frosting (page 98).

If you'd like to make your own baking powder, ½ teaspoon of cream of tartar plus ¼ teaspoon of baking soda will equal 1 teaspoon of baking powder. You can also substitute the same amount of baking soda for baking powder in this recipe.

1½ cups (144 g) almond flour

¼ cup (20 g) cocoa powder

¼ teaspoon salt

1 teaspoon baking powder

¼ cup plus 2 tablespoons low-carb 1:1 sweetener, or equivalent (see chart on page 15)

¼ cup (60 ml) olive oil

½ cup (120 ml) almond milk (or other milk)

2 large eggs

1 tablespoon (15 ml) vanilla extract

1. Preheat your oven to 325°F (170°C, or gas mark 3).

2. Prepare a muffin pan with 8 cupcake liners.

3. Whisk the almond flour, cocoa powder, salt, and baking powder together in a bowl.

4. Add the sweetener, olive oil, milk, eggs, and vanilla, and mix until well blended.

5. Fill the cupcake liners until three-fourths full with batter and bake for 25 minutes, or until a toothpick inserted into the center of a cupcake comes out clean.

6. Cool and frost if desired. Store covered at room temperature for a week or so, or store in the refrigerator for a few weeks.

YIELD: 8 cupcakes

PER SERVING: 122 calories; 4 g carbohydrate; 2 g fat; 3 g protein; 2 g fiber

TIRAMISU

•DAIRY-FREE OPTION   •GRAIN-FREE   •GLUTEN-FREE

This Italian coffee-flavored dessert is traditionally made with ladyfinger cookies, but I like to make it with Yellow Cake (page 79) baked in an 8 × 8-inch (20 × 20-cm) baking dish, if possible, to make a square cake. Tiramisu does require some planning because it tastes best when it is assembled and then placed in the refrigerator overnight to give the coffee time to soak into the cake and cream.

To make this dairy-free, use Coconut Whipped Cream (page 100) in place of the heavy cream and eliminate the mascarpone cheese. Using just heavy cream or coconut cream makes it a bit lighter and reduces the amount of fat and carbs.

8 ounces (225 g) mascarpone cheese

⅓ cup low-carb 1:1 sweetener, or equivalent (see chart on page 15)

1 cup (235 ml) heavy cream

1 cup (235 ml) dark brewed coffee, at room temperature, divided

1 recipe Yellow Cake (page 79), baked in a square pan and cooled

¼ cup (25 g) unsweetened cocoa powder, divided

1. Place the mascarpone cheese and sweetener in a mixing bowl (or use a handheld mixer) and beat until well blended. Add the heavy cream and mix until well combined and fluffy.

2. Slice the cake layer in half and place one half on the bottom of an 8 × 8-inch (20 × 20-cm) dish.

3. Drip half of the coffee evenly over the cake.

4. Spread half of the cheese and cream mixture over the cake.

5. Sprinkle or sift half of the cocoa powder evenly over the cream layer.

6. Place the other half of the cake on top of the cocoa.

7. Drip the remaining coffee evenly over the cake.

8. Spread the remaining cream over the cake and sprinkle with the remaining cocoa powder.

9. Cover the dish and place in the refrigerator overnight. Serve chilled.

YIELD: 16 servings

PER SERVING: 331 calories; 11 g carbohydrate; 30 g fat; 5 g protein; 0 g fiber

CINNAMON STREUSEL CAKE (OR LOAF)

•DAIRY-FREE OPTION   •NUT-FREE   •GRAIN-FREE   •GLUTEN-FREE

This recipe is based on the Cinnamon Bun Muffins (page 61) with a bit of shifting in the amount of sweetener and the addition of coconut milk. Sometimes I just want one loaf to slice up and store as a whole, and this recipe is just that.

As for the baking pan size, you have some flexibility here. You can use either a 7.5 × 3.5 × 2.25-inch (19 × 9 × 7-cm) loaf pan or an 8 × 8 × 2-inch (20 x 20 x 5-cm) square cake pan.

Make this dairy-free by replacing the yogurt with coconut milk or other dairy-free milk.

FOR THE LOAF:

½ cup (52 g) coconut flour

¼ teaspoon baking soda

¼ teaspoon salt

4 large eggs

⅓ cup (77 g) yogurt or dairy-free milk

⅓ cup low-carb 1:1 sweetener, or equivalent (see chart on page 15)

2 tablespoons (30 ml) coconut milk or other milk

FOR THE STREUSEL TOPPING:

2 tablespoons (14 g) ground cinnamon

¼ cup low-carb 1:1 sweetener, or equivalent (see chart on page 15)

2 tablespoons (28 g) unsalted butter, melted

⅓ cup (40 g) chopped walnuts or pecans (optional)

1. Preheat oven to 350°F (180°C, or gas mark 4).

2. Grease the baking pan (see above) well, or line the bottom with parchment paper and grease the sides; dust with a small amount of coconut flour.

3. **To make the loaf:** Whisk the flour, baking soda, and salt together in a bowl.

4. Add the eggs, yogurt, sweetener, and coconut milk to the flour mixture and blend well, using a mixer or a food processor. Let the batter sit for a few minutes.

5. **To make the streusel topping:** Place the cinnamon, sweetener, butter, and walnuts in a small bowl and mix together with a fork or whisk.

6. Scoop the batter into the baking pan and then pour the topping over the batter. Use a fork to swirl the topping around the batter.

7. Bake the loaf for 40 minutes, or until a toothpick inserted in the center comes out clean.

8. Cool and slice.

YIELD: 1 loaf, or 8 servings

PER SERVING: 100 calories; 12 g carbohydrate; 6 g fat; 4 g protein; 3 g fiber

VANILLA CUPCAKES

•DAIRY-FREE OPTION   •NUT-FREE   •GRAIN-FREE   •GLUTEN-FREE

Just in case you don't like chocolate or just need a change, here are simple and reliable vanilla cupcakes. I've used this recipe as a base for several others, and it can withstand a number of variations and additions.

To make it dairy-free, use coconut oil or olive oil instead of butter, and to make the cupcake richer, replace the milk with heavy cream or coconut cream.

½ cup (52 g) coconut flour

¼ teaspoon baking soda

¼ teaspoon salt

4 large eggs

⅓ cup (76 g) unsalted butter, melted

½ cup low-carb 1:1 sweetener, or equivalent (see chart on page 15)

1 tablespoon (15 ml) vanilla extract

2 tablespoons (30 ml) coconut milk or other milk

1. Preheat your oven to 350°F (180°C, or gas mark 4).

2. Prepare a cupcake pan with cupcake liners.

3. Add the coconut flour, baking soda, and salt to a bowl and blend well.

4. In a separate bowl, whisk together the eggs, butter, sweetener, vanilla, and coconut milk. Add this mixture to the dry ingredients and use a handheld or stand mixer to blend well. Let the batter sit for a few minutes and then mix once more.

5. Fill the cupcake liners about three-quarters of the way with batter and bake for 20 minutes, or until a toothpick inserted in the center of a cupcake comes out clean.

6. Cool and frost. Store the cupcakes, covered, at room temperature for a few days, in the refrigerator for a few weeks, or in the freezer for a few months.

YIELD: 8 cupcakes

PER SERVING: 138 calories; 10 g carbohydrate; 11 g fat; 4 g protein; 3 g fiber

HOW TO MAKE BEET JUICE

Beet juice is the ultimate natural food coloring. It's naturally sweet, a bit earthy, and a great source of essential vitamins and minerals. I make beet juice with a juicer, or you can blend steamed beets and then strain the juice from them.

First prepare the beets by cleaning off any soil or debris, trim and peel any roots and stems, and finally peel off the outer skin. Chop the beets up into pieces. For the juicer method, add the beet pieces to your juicer to extract the juices. For the blender method, steam the beets for 30 minutes, and then place the beet pieces in your blender along with about ¼ cup (60 ml) water, and blend. Strain the juice from the pulp using cheesecloth or a nut milk bag.

One caution: Beet juice stains some materials, including clothing, so take care not to get it on your clothes or any porous surfaces.

RED VELVET CUPCAKES

•DAIRY-FREE   •NUT-FREE   •GRAIN-FREE   •GLUTEN-FREE

Red velvet cake and cupcakes are typically dark red or reddish-brown in color, thanks to the cocoa and artificial food coloring. I prefer to use red beet juice to get a rich reddish-brown color for this cupcake, but in a pinch you can use 1 to 2 tablespoons (15 to 30 ml) of natural red food dye (see reources, page 154). The beet juice also lends moistness and flavor to the cupcake. You'll notice I also add yogurt and lemon juice to add acidity that will maintain the red color of the beet juice while it bakes. The yogurt also lends additional moistness to the cupcake's texture and helps it rise.

Traditionally, red velvet cupcakes and cake are frosted with cream cheese frosting, so try Maple Cream Cheese Frosting (page 100) or Dairy-Free Maple Cream Frosting (page 101). To make this dairy-free, substitute coconut milk for the yogurt or use a dairy-free yogurt.

½ cup (52 g) coconut flour

2 tablespoons (11 g) unsweetened cocoa powder

½ teaspoon salt

¼ teaspoon baking soda

4 large eggs

2 tablespoons (30 ml) olive oil or other oil

½ cup low-carb 1:1 sweetener, or equivalent (see chart on page 15)

1 tablespoon (15 g) plain yogurt or sour cream

1 teaspoon vanilla extract

2 tablespoons (30 ml) lemon juice

2 tablespoons (30 ml) beet juice (about 1 medium red beet; see sidebar)

Frosting of your choice (see headnote)

1. Preheat your oven to 350°F (180°C, or gas mark 4).

2. Line a cupcake pan with cupcake liners or use silicone cupcake liners. Even if you're using parchment paper liners I suggest greasing the liners for this recipe to prevent the cupcakes from sticking.

3. Whisk the coconut flour, cocoa, salt, and baking soda together in a bowl.

4. Whisk the eggs, oil, sweetener, yogurt, vanilla, and lemon juice and then add the mixture to the dry ingredients and mix, using a handheld or stand mixer. Add the beet juice and mix again. Let the batter sit for a few minutes and mix once more.

5. Fill the cupcake liners three-quarters of the way with batter. Tap the pan gently to even out the batter in the liners.

6. Bake for 20 minutes, or until a toothpick inserted in the center comes out clean.

7. Cool and frost. Store, covered, at room temperature for a few days, in the refrigerator for a few weeks, or in the freezer for a few months.

YIELD: 8 cupcakes

PER SERVING: Calories: 104 calories; 11 g carbohydrate; 7 g fat; 4 g protein; 3 g fiber

CHOCOLATE CUPCAKES

•GLUTEN-FREE　•GRAIN-FREE　•DAIRY-FREE

Perfect for an everyday muffin or cupcake, these light and fluffy chocolate cupcakes are not too sweet and go exceptionally well with Whipped Chocolate Frosting (page 96). I also like to add chocolate chips to them. To prevent the chips from sinking to the bottom of the thin batter, use only about ½ cup (84 g) chocolate chips and add a few to each cupcake after you've filled the cupcake liner. I sprinkle them across each cupcake and then shuffle the cupcake pan back and forth to allow the chips to sink a bit into the batter.

¼ cup (26 g) coconut flour

¼ cup (20 g) unsweetened cocoa

¼ teaspoon salt

¼ teaspoon baking soda

3 large eggs

½ cup low-carb 1:1 sweetener, or equivalent (see chart on page 15)

½ cup coconut milk or other milk

1. Preheat your oven to 350°F (180°C, or gas mark 4).

2. Prepare a cupcake pan with parchment cupcake liners.

3. Add the coconut flour, cocoa, salt, and baking soda to a bowl and blend well.

4. Whisk the eggs, sweetener, and milk together, then add the mixture to the dry ingredients and mix using a handheld or stand mixer until well blended. Let the batter sit for a few minutes and mix once more. This batter is somewhat thin, so don't be alarmed if it doesn't thicken like some other muffin and cupcake batters.

5. Fill each cupcake liner halfway with batter. Bake for about 15 minutes, or until a toothpick inserted in the center of a cupcake comes out clean.

6. Cool and frost. Store in a sealed container at room temperature for a few days, in the refrigerator for a few weeks, or in the freezer for a few months.

YIELD: 8 cupcakes

PER SERVING: 51 calories; 9 g carbohydrate; 3 g fat; 3 g protein; 2 g fiber

CHOCOLATE GANACHE AND WHIPPED CHOCOLATE FROSTING

·NUT-FREE   **·EGG-FREE**   **·GRAIN-FREE**   **·GLUTEN-FREE**

Whipping cream with sweetened chocolate results in a light, creamy chocolate frosting that is perfect for cupcakes and cakes. This frosting works well for Chocolate Cupcakes (page 81), but it goes just as well on just about any cupcake or cake. Or eat it straight up with a spoon, as I've been known to do.

There are actually two recipes here: Chocolate Ganache and Whipped Chocolate Frosting. You'll have ganache after you've melted the chocolate in the heavy cream. At this point you can cool the mixture and then spread it across cakes or cupcakes (it's great as a frosting for Chocolate Layer Cake on page 83), or take it to the next level and whip it, and you'll have a light, creamy chocolate frosting that resembles chocolate buttercream frosting.

1 cup (235 ml) heavy cream

1½ cups (252 g) sugar-free chocolate chips

Pinch salt (less than ⅛ teaspoon)

1. Place the cream in a saucepan, bring to a soft boil, and then turn off the heat.

2. Add the chocolate to the cream and stir to dissolve.

3. Cool to room temperature. The longer it cools, the thicker it will get. You can chill it a few minutes in the refrigerator to speed up the cooling process. You can then use it as a ganache or make whipped frosting.

4. To use it as ganache, chill it in the refrigerator until it's thick enough to pour or to spread as frosting.

5. **To make the whipped chocolate frosting:** use a whisk or handheld or stand mixer to whip the mixture for a few minutes until it becomes light and creamy. It can be stored in a sealed container in the refrigerator for a few days. Frost with the whipped chocolate when it is at room temperature.

YIELD: About 2 cups (490 g), or 8 servings

PER SERVING: 313 calories; 13 g carbohydrate; 25 g fat; 4 g protein; 3 g fiber

MAKE YOUR OWN PASTRY BAG

If you don't have a pastry bag, you can convert a Ziploc bag into one. Simply place the bag halfway into a cup and scoop the frosting into the bag. Lift the bag out of the cup, seal, and guide the frosting toward the bottom of one corner of the bag. Snip off a tiny piece of the corner and start piping!

DAIRY-FREE CHOCOLATE GANACHE

•GLUTEN-FREE   •GRAIN-FREE   •DAIRY-FREE   •NUT-FREE
•EGG-FREE

Here's a simple ganache recipe that can be made in one saucepan in 5 minutes. Yes, it's that simple. The coconut oil makes it dairy-free, but you can use butter if dairy isn't an issue. If you're using this for a layer cake, you'll want to double the recipe to cover both layers.

¼ cup (60 ml) coconut oil

¼ cup (20 g) unsweetened cocoa powder

2 tablespoons low-carb 1:1 sweetener, or equivalent (see chart on page 15)

½ teaspoon vanilla

Pinch salt (less than ⅛ teaspoon)

1. Melt the coconut oil in a small saucepan over a low heat. It won't take long for the oil to melt because it has a low melting point, which is why it's sometimes a liquid in your pantry during hot summer days.

2. Turn the heat off and stir in the cocoa powder, sweetener, vanilla, and salt.

3. Let the ganache cool to room temperature or, to speed things up, place the saucepan in the refrigerator for about 5 minutes.

4. Spoon or drizzle the ganache over cupcakes, cakes, muffins, and cookies. Let it cool at room temperature for 5 minutes or so, or refrigerate until ready to devour.

5. You can store the ganache in a sealed container in the refrigerator for a few weeks. Reheat on a low heat to use it again.

YIELD: About ½ cup (134 g), or 8 servings

PER SERVING: 313 calories; 13 g carbohydrate; 25 g fat; 4 g protein; 3 g fiber

CHOCOLATE BUTTERCREAM FROSTING

•NUT-FREE   •EGG-FREE
•GRAIN-FREE   •GLUTEN-FREE

½ cup (114 g) unsalted butter, softened

2 tablespoons low-carb 1:1 sweetener, or equivalent (see chart on page 15)

½ cup (40 g) unsweetened cocoa powder

1 teaspoon vanilla extract

Pinch salt

1. Place the butter and sweetener in a mixing bowl and mix using a handheld or stand mixer until the butter begins to get creamy.

2. Add the sweetener, cocoa, vanilla, and salt and mix for a few minutes or until the frosting is creamy.

3. Frost at room temperature.

YIELD: About ¾ cup (235 g), or 8 servings

PER SERVING: 313 calories; 13 g carbohydrate; 25 g fat; 4 g protein; 3 g fiber

CHOCOLATE FROSTING

•NUT-FREE   •EGG-FREE
•GRAIN-FREE   •GLUTEN-FREE

This is a classic chocolate frosting that is very easy to whip up. It frosts about 12 cupcakes or a one-layer cake. I recommend doubling it for a two-layer cake.

You can use unsweetened chocolate and a low-carb sweetener to make this, or you can use low-carb sweetened chocolate chips, like Lily's brand. See reources on page 154 for more information.

1 cup (240 ml) heavy cream

12 ounces (340 g) sugar-free chocolate

1. Place the cream in a saucepan and bring it to a soft boil over medium heat.

2. Turn off the heat and add the chocolate to the cream. Stir until the chocolate is dissolved.

3. Cool the frosting to room temperature. You can also chill in the refrigerator for faster results.

4. Using a whip attachment on a handheld or standing mixer, whip the frosting for a few minutes until it is light and creamy.

5. Store covered in the refrigerator for a week or so.

YIELD: 2 cups (480 g), or 12 servings

PER SERVING: 180 calories; 11 g carbohydrate; 15 g fat; 2 g protein; 3 g fiber

VANILLA BUTTERCREAM FROSTING

•NUT-FREE •EGG-FREE
•GRAIN-FREE •GLUTEN-FREE

Here's creamy vanilla frosting that can be used to frost 12 cupcakes or a two-layer cake.

I recommend using a low-carb powdered sweetener, such as Swerve, Lakanto, or NOW brand erythritol. See resources on page 154 for more information.

1 cup (2 sticks, or 230 g) unsalted butter, at room temperature

2 tablespoons (30 ml) whipping cream or milk

2 teaspoons vanilla extract

½ cup low-carb 1:1 powdered sweetener, or equivalent (see headnote and chart on page 15)

1. Place all the ingredients in a bowl and mix well with an electric or hand mixer until well combined and creamy, about 1 minute.

2. Store covered in the refrigerator for a few days.

YIELD: 1½ cups (360 g), or 12 servings

PER SERVING: 77 calories; 0 g carbohydrate; 9 g fat; 0 g protein; 0 g fiber

MAPLE WHIPPED CREAM

•GLUTEN-FREE •GRAIN-FREE
•LOW-SUGAR OPTION
•NUT-FREE •EGG-FREE

Sugar-free maple syrup is the sweetener for this recipe; however, feel free to use another liquid or crystal low-carb sweetener to create whipped cream. This recipe makes enough to frost 8 cupcakes, so if you want to use it to frost a two-layer cake, double the recipe.

1 cup (235 ml) heavy cream

1 to 2 tablespoons (21 to 42 g) sugar-free maple syrup

Add the cream and maple syrup to a bowl or mixing bowl and use a whisk attachment on a handheld or stand mixer to whip the cream until it becomes light and the peaks are stiff. This will take a few minutes.

YIELD: About 2 cups (268 g), or 8 servings

PER SERVING: 103 calories; 1 g carbohydrate; 11 g fat; 1 g protein; 3 g fiber

COCONUT WHIPPED CREAM

- •GLUTEN-FREE •GRAIN-FREE
- •DAIRY-FREE •LOW-SUGAR
- •NUT-FREE •EGG-FREE

Coconut cream can be used as a substitute for dairy-based cream in many recipes. The trick to getting coconut cream from coconut milk is to refrigerate the full-fat coconut milk (24 hours is best) so that the cream separates out while chilling. Then you skim the cream off the top. Another option is to purchase coconut cream (see resources, page 154). My favorite brand of coconut milk and coconut cream is Aroy-D because it has no additives.

1 pint (473 ml) coconut milk with the cream

1 teaspoon low-carb 1:1 sweetener, or equivalent (see chart on page 15)

1. Place the coconut milk in the refrigerator for 24 hours.

2. Gently skim the cream off the top of the coconut milk without taking any liquid below it.

3. Place the cream and sweetener in a mixing bowl and whip it using a handheld or stand mixer.

4. Store, covered, in the refrigerator for a few days and rewhip as necessary.

YIELD: ½ cup (234 g), or 4 servings

PER SERVING: 280 calories; 8 g carbohydrate; 29 g fat; 3 g protein; 3 g fiber

MAPLE CREAM CHEESE FROSTING

- •NUT-FREE •EGG-FREE
- •GRAIN-FREE •GLUTEN-FREE

This creamy, sweet, and slightly tangy frosting is easy to make and store in the refrigerator until you're ready to use it. It goes well with Pumpkin Bread (page 48) and can also be used to frost a two-layer cake. Look for a cream cheese that doesn't have additives, and if you can't find one, use fromage blanc (farmer's cheese) or dripped (Greek) yogurt for this recipe.

1 pound (455 g) cream cheese or fromage blanc

½ cup (170 g) sugar-free maple syrup

Combine all the ingredients in a bowl and whisk until fully blended.

YIELD: About 1½ cups (625 g), or 12 servings

PER SERVING: 416 calories; 5 g carbohydrate; 41 g fat; 7 g protein; 0 g fiber

DAIRY-FREE MAPLE CREAM FROSTING

•DAIRY-FREE   •EGG-FREE
•GRAIN-FREE   •GLUTEN-FREE

This frosting can be used on just about any muffin, cake, or cupcake. It does require a bit of planning—you'll need about 3 hours to soak the cashews until they are soft enough to yield a creamy frosting.

1 cup (110 g) raw cashews, soaked in water for 3 hours

½ cup (120 ml) apple juice

2 teaspoons (10 ml) lemon juice

¼ cup low-carb 1:1 sweetener, or equivalent (see chart on page 15)

2 teaspoons (10 ml) vanilla extract

Pinch salt (up to ⅛ teaspoon)

1. Place all the ingredients in a high-speed blender or food processor and blend until creamy.

2. Store in a sealed container in the refrigerator for a week or so.

YIELD: About 2 cups (300 g), or 12 servings

PER SERVING: 64 calories; 7 g carbohydrate; 4 g fat; 2 g protein; 0 g fiber

BROWNIES

·DAIRY-FREE OPTION   **·GRAIN-FREE**   **·GLUTEN-FREE**

These are light, cakelike brownies that work well with low-carb sweeteners that have bulk to them (see the chart on page 15). They taste great with or without frosting, but to make them even more decadent, use Chocolate Frosting on page 98.

To make this dairy-free, replace the butter with coconut oil.

½ cup (48 g) almond flour

⅓ cup (30 g) unsweetened cocoa powder

⅔ cup low-carb 1:1 sweetener, or equivalent (see headnote and chart on page 15)

½ teaspoon salt

½ teaspoon baking powder

½ teaspoon vanilla extract

½ cup (112 g) unsalted butter, melted

3 large eggs

1. Preheat your oven to 350°F (180°C, or gas mark 4).

2. Lightly grease an 8 × 8-inch (20 × 20-cm) baking pan.

3. Add the dry ingredients to a bowl and whisk until well blended.

4. Add the wet ingredients to the dry ingredients and whisk to blend well.

5. Pour the batter into the prepared baking pan and use a spatula to spread it evenly.

6. Bake for 15 minutes, or until a toothpick inserted into the center comes out mostly clean.

7. Cool and slice into 16 squares.

YIELD: 16 servings

PER SERVING: 109 calories; 10 g carbohydrate; 7 g fat; 2 g protein; 1 g fiber

EGG-FREE AND DAIRY-FREE OPTIONS

To make this egg-free, replace the egg with 1 tablespoon (7 g) flax-seed meal + 3 tablespoons (45 ml) water. Mix the flaxseed and water together first, let it sit for a minute, and then add it to the batter.

To make this dairy-free, use coconut oil in place of the butter or ghee.

CHOCOLATE CHIP COOKIES

•GLUTEN-FREE   •GRAIN-FREE   •DAIRY-FREE OPTION
•EGG-FREE OPTION

This is a great cookie dough recipe to have around whenever you're craving a soft cookie. You make the dough and freeze it; then, when you want fresh-baked cookies, remove the dough from the freezer, slice up the cookies, and pop them in the oven. The dough will keep well in the freezer for several months.

If you don't want to freeze the dough and slice it, you can instead shape them by hand. Roll about a tablespoon of dough in your hands, place the ball on the baking mat and flatten the dough ball down with the inside of your palm to shape the cookie; repeat for each cookie.

¼ cup (55 g) unsalted butter, or ghee softened

⅓ cup low-carb 1:1 sweetener, or equivalent (see chart on page 15)

1 large egg

2 teaspoons vanilla extract

1½ cups (144 g) blanched almond flour

2 tablespoons (13 g) coconut flour

¼ teaspoon baking soda

¼ teaspoon salt

½ cup (84g) sugar-free chocolate chips (see reources on page 154)

1. Add the butter, sweetener, egg, and vanilla to a bowl and mix until well blended. A stand or handheld mixer works well. This mixture won't become creamy.

2. Whisk the almond flour, coconut flour, baking soda, and salt together in a separate bowl, then add it to the wet batter and mix well. Stir in the chocolate chips.

3. At this point you can freeze the dough then slice it, or skip ahead and preheat the oven, shape the dough by hand (see above), and bake. To freeze the dough, add it to one end of the paper and roll the dough in a cylinder until covered. Twist the ends of the paper to simultaneously push the dough closer together and to close each end.

4. Preheat oven to 350°F (180°C, or gas mark 4).

5. Unroll the dough, slice the cookies about ¼ inch (6 mm) thick, and place them on baking sheets lined with parchment paper or on a nonstick baking mat. Space them about ½ inch (13 mm) apart, since they don't spread while baking.

6. Bake for 12 to 15 minutes, or until they are just starting to turn golden.

YIELD: About 20 cookies

PER SERVING: 104 calories; 5 g carbohydrate; 9 g fat; 3 g protein; 2 g fiber

SNICKERDOODLES

˙EGG-FREE   ˙GRAIN-FREE   ˙GLUTEN-FREE

Snickerdoodles are traditionally cinnamon sugar cookies that have a chewy bite to them. The combination of almond flour and coconut flour for this version creates a nice balance of sweetness, spice, and buttery flavor. For the topping, I recommend using granulated low-carb sweetener to get the effect of using sugar. These cookies get soft after a day or so, so if you want to regain the crunchy edges, pop them in a warm oven or in a dehydrator for several minutes.

2 cups (192 g) blanched almond flour

2 tablespoons (13 g) coconut flour

¼ teaspoon baking soda

¼ teaspoon salt

3 tablespoons (42 g) unsalted butter, melted

⅓ cup low-carb 1:1 sweetener, or equivalent (see chart on page 15)

¼ cup (60 ml) coconut milk

1 tablespoon (15 ml) vanilla extract

2 tablespoons (14 g) ground cinnamon

2 tablespoons low-carb granulated 1:1 sweetener, or equivalent (see chart on page 15)

1. Preheat oven to 350°F (180°C, or gas mark 4).

2. Whisk together the almond flour, coconut flour, baking soda, and salt in a bowl.

3. In a separate bowl, cream the butter, sweetener, and vanilla.

4. Add the flour mixture to the butter mixture and blend well. If the batter is a bit soft to handle, chill it for 10 minutes.

5. Line baking sheets with a nonstick mat, parchment paper, or another nonstick material.

6. Blend the ground cinnamon and low-carb granulated sweetener together in a shallow bowl or plate. Using the palms of your hands, roll a tablespoon or so of dough into a ball. Roll the dough ball in the cinnamon mixture to fully coat. Place the dough balls on the cookie sheet, spaced about an inch (2.5 cm) or so apart, and flatten with the underside of a jar or glass, or with the palm of your hand.

7. Bake the cookies for 8 to 10 minutes. Cool for at least 10 minutes.

8. Store in a sealed container at room temperature for a few days or in the freezer for a few months.

YIELD: 20 cookies

PER SERVING: 86 calories; 3 g carbohydrate; 7 g fat; 3 g protein; 2 g fiber

CHEESECAKE BROWNIES

·NUT-FREE ·GRAIN-FREE ·DAIRY-FREE OPTION ·GLUTEN-FREE

Cheesecake brownies combine the thick chocolate texture of a brownie with the creamy richness of cheese.

For the cheese layer, you have a few options: Try yogurt instead of cream cheese if you're a fan. You can make this dairy-free using coconut oil in place of butter and dairy-free cream cheese or yogurt.

FOR THE BROWNIE LAYER:

1 recipe Brownies (page 105), unbaked

FOR THE CHEESECAKE LAYER:

8 ounces (225 g) cream cheese, at room temperature

¼ cup low-carb 1:1 sweetener, or equivalent (see chart on page 15)

1 teaspoon vanilla extract

1 large egg

1. Preheat your oven to 350°F (180°C or gas mark 4).

2. Line the bottom of an 8 × 8-inch (20 × 20-cm) baking pan with parchment paper, or grease it generously.

3. **To make the brownie layer:** Make the batter using the recipe on page 105.

4. **To make the cheesecake layer:** In a separate bowl, combine the cream cheese, sweetener, vanilla, and egg, and mix until blended.

5. Pour the brownie batter into the baking pan. Next, pour the cheesecake batter on top of the brownie batter. Use a toothpick to swirl the cheesecake batter into the brownie batter.

6. Bake for 20 minutes, or until a toothpick inserted in the middle of the brownies comes out clean.

7. Cool fully before slicing. These taste even better cold. Store in the refrigerator for a week or so.

YIELD: 16 squares

PER SERVING: 129 calories; 2 g carbohydrate; 13 g fat; 3 g protein; 1 g fiber

TRIPLE BERRY COBBLER

·DAIRY-FREE   ·EGG-FREE   ·GRAIN-FREE   ·GLUTEN-FREE

Triple berry can become double berry or even quadruple berry depending on what's in season or what you have in your freezer. My mix usually includes blueberries, raspberries, and strawberries. You can vary the ratio of berries depending on the balance of sweetness and tartness of your berries. If using frozen berries, first thaw them completely and drain any excess liquid.

You'll notice I don't use cornstarch to thicken the berry mixture, but you can add 1 tablespoon (6 g) almond flour to thicken the filling, or boil the filling in a saucepan over medium heat for about 10 minutes, cool it a few minutes, and then pour it into your baking dish and top it with the cobbler crust. You can use a pie plate or baking dish to make this cobbler; I tend to use a 9-inch (23-cm) pie plate and treat it as a one-crust pie.

2 pounds (1 kg) berries (about 5 cups, or 2½ pints)

¼ cup low-carb 1:1 sweetener, or equivalent (see chart on page 15)

¼ teaspoon salt

¼ teaspoon ground cinnamon

1 tablespoon (15 ml) lemon juice

2 tablespoons (30 ml) egg white (about ½ large egg white) (optional)

1 recipe Almond Cobbler and Pie Crust (page 118)

1. Preheat your oven to 350°F (180°C, or gas mark 4).

2. Combine the berries, sweetener, salt, cinnamon, and lemon juice in a bowl and blend gently with a spoon or spatula.

3. Scoop the berry filling into a pie plate or baking dish.

4. Place the cobbler crust between two pieces of parchment paper and roll it out to the size that fits over the baking dish, and place it on top of the filling. Pinch the corners with your fingers to seal the crust around the edges. Brush the egg white over the crust and poke holes in the crust with fork.

5. Place the cobbler in the oven and place a baking sheet under it to catch any drips. Bake for 30 minutes, or until the filling is bubbling and the crust is browned.

6. Cool for a few minutes and serve. Store at room temperature for a few days or in the refrigerator for a week or so.

YIELD: 1 pie, or 8 servings

PER SERVING: 171 calories; 16 g carbohydrate; 13 g fat; 5 g protein; 1 g fiber

COWBOY QUICHE

·NUT-FREE OPTION   ·GRAIN-FREE   ·GLUTEN-FREE

I'm a city kid by birth, but since moving to the West Coast I've grown to appreciate the cowboy and cowgirl culture. I was inspired by a couple of recipes I've seen by the same name to create this recipe. I suspect cowboys and cowgirls of all ages will love this one, especially anyone who loves a hardy breakfast in a single slice of goodness. For the sausage, you can use bulk chicken, pork, or turkey sausage, or take sausage out of its casings. Another option is to use 8 slices of bacon, chopped into pieces, in place of the sausage. Use your favorite cheese, stay with cheddar, or mix it up with some Monterey Jack cheese.

2 tablespoons (28 g) ghee, unsalted butter, coconut oil, or other oil

1 large yellow onion, sliced into thin strips

½ pound (227 g) bulk seasoned sausage

6 large eggs

⅓ cup (77 g) yogurt, sour cream, or heavy cream

1½ cups (170 g) shredded sharp cheddar cheese or other cheese

¼ teaspoon salt

Dash Tabasco sauce or pinch cayenne pepper

Salt and pepper

1 recipe Everyday Pie Crust (page 115) for a nut-free option, Pastry Crust (page 117), or Almond Cobbler and Pie Crust (page 118)

1. Preheat a skillet on a medium heat and add the ghee and onions. Cook the onions, stirring occasionally, for 10 minutes, or until they begin to caramelize. Place the onions in a large mixing bowl.

2. Add the sausage to the skillet and cook over medium heat for 5 minutes, or until it's browned and almost completely cooked.

3. Add the sausage to the onions, and stir in the eggs, yogurt, cheese, salt, and Tabasco sauce. Season with salt and pepper.

4. Press the pie crust into an 8-inch (20-cm) or 9-inch (23-cm) pie or tart pan. Add the sausage mixture and bake for 30 minutes, or until the center of the quiche is cooked and not transparent.

5. Cool for a minute and serve. Store, covered, in the refrigerator for a few days or in the freezer for a few months.

YIELD: 1 quiche, or 8 servings

PER SERVING: 350 calories; 7 g carbohydrate; 16 g fat; 13 g protein; 0 g fiber

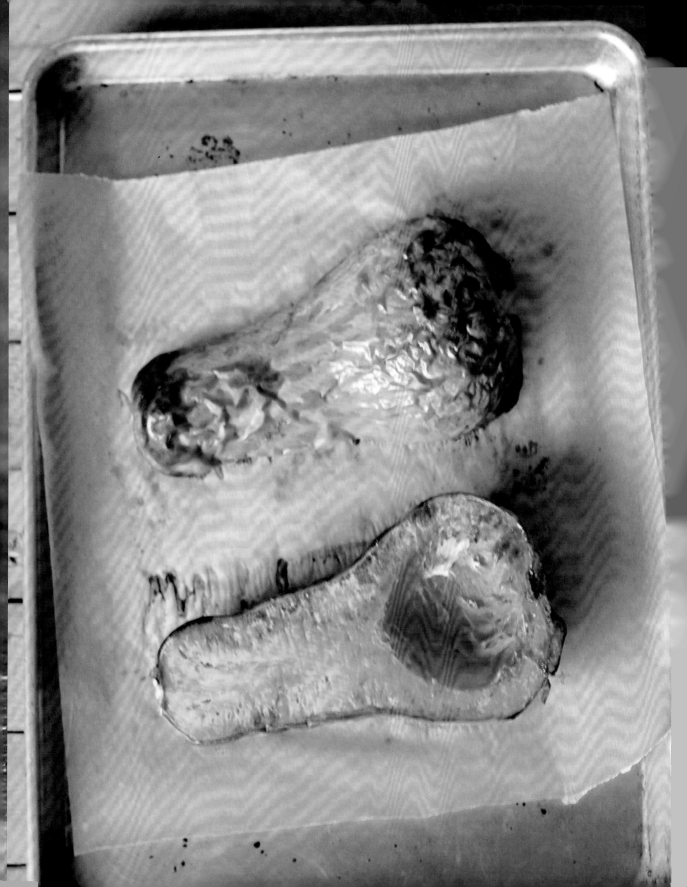

ROASTED BUTTERNUT SQUASH SOUP

·DAIRY-FREE OPTION   ·NUT-FREE   ·EGG-FREE   ·GRAIN-FREE
·GLUTEN-FREE

Butternut squash offers a solid punch of the vitamins found in orange-colored foods. It's loaded with vitamin A and C, with some iron and calcium thrown in for good measure. Unlike citrus fruits with a similar vitamin profile, it's not acidic, which makes it quite gentle on sensitive digestive systems. And another amazing fact? Butternut squash seems to last for months without going bad—I've used one up to 3 months old.

2 tablespoons (28 g) unsalted butter, ghee, or coconut oil

1 medium yellow onion, peeled and diced

2½ cups (600 ml) Chicken Broth (page 133), vegetable broth, or water

4 large garlic cloves, peeled and minced

3 cups (720 g) roasted butternut squash (see below), warmed

1. Preheat a skillet on medium heat and add the butter. Add the onions to the skillet and cook, stirring occasionally, until they begin to brown and caramelize.

2. In the meantime, bring the broth to a simmer in a saucepan over low heat. Then place the garlic in the pan and cook another few minutes, or until the garlic becomes fragrant.

3. Place the butternut squash, onions, garlic, and chicken broth in a blender and blend until smooth.

4. Serve warm. Store in a sealed container in the refrigerator for a few days or in the freezer for a few months.

YIELD: 4 servings

PER SERVING: 232 calories; 28 g carbohydrate; 10 g fat; 5 g protein; 4 g fiber

HOW TO ROAST BUTTERNUT SQUASH

Here's a simple method for making roasted squash that can be used in this recipe as well as the Spiced Pumpkin Bread on page 48.

Preheat your oven to 400°F (200°C, or gas mark 6). Slice one butternut squash in half lengthwise, and then scoop out the seeds. Rub the inside of each squash half with coconut oil, ghee, or other high-heat oil, and place on a greased or parchment-lined baking sheet, cut side up. Roast for about 30 minutes, or until the squash is tender and you can insert a fork in the thickest part.

Cool, and then cut into cubes for recipes needing diced cooked squash. To make purée, scoop out the squash and purée it in a blender. If it's dry you may need to add a bit of water. Leftover squash may be kept in a sealed container in the refrigerator for a few days or in the freezer for a few months.

SCALLION CHICKEN PANCAKES

•DAIRY-FREE   •NUT-FREE   •GRAIN-FREE   •GLUTEN-FREE

In this recipe the coconut flour is a supporting player, helping to thicken the patties to balance out the moist additions of sesame oil and soy sauce. They make a great appetizer or side.

FOR THE SOY GINGER SAUCE:

¼ cup 1:1 sweetener, or equivalent (see chart on page 15)

¼ cup (60 ml) water

¼ cup (60 ml) gluten-free soy sauce

2 tablespoons (12 g) chopped fresh ginger

½ teaspoon ground coriander

FOR THE PANCAKES:

5 scallions

1 cup (16 g) cilantro or other herb, such as arugula or parsley

1 pound (454 g) ground chicken, pork, or turkey

1 large egg

2 tablespoons (30 ml) toasted sesame oil

2 tablespoons (30 ml) gluten-free soy sauce or ½ teaspoon salt

1 tablespoon (7 g) coconut flour

2 tablespoons (30 ml) cooking oil, for cooking

1. **To make the soy ginger sauce:** Add the sweetener, water, soy sauce, ginger, and coriander to a saucepan and simmer for 30 minutes, or until the liquid is reduced by about half.

2. Cool the sauce and pour it through a fine-mesh strainer to remove the ginger and coriander. The sauce will be slightly thickened and syrupy when cooled.

3. **To make the pancakes:** Finely mince the scallions and cilantro.

4. Add the scallions, cilantro, and chicken to a bowl and mix well.

5. Add the egg, sesame oil, soy sauce, and coconut flour to the chicken mixture and blend well.

6. Preheat a large skillet over medium heat and add the cooking oil. Using an ice cream scoop or large spoon, scoop out 1 to 2 tablespoons (between 14 and 28 g) of the chicken mixture and drop into skillet. Flatten a bit with the spoon to create a small pancake. Cook each pancake about 5 minutes on each side, or until they are browning.

7. Place cooked pancakes on a paper towel over a warm plate and continue with the remaining batter.

8. Serve warm with soy ginger sauce. Store in a sealed container in the refrigerator for a few days or in the freezer for a few weeks. The sauce can be stored, covered, in the refrigerator for several weeks.

YIELD: About 16 pancakes, or 3 to 4 servings

PER SERVING: 268 calories; 4 g carbohydrate; 16 g fat; 29 g protein; 1 g fiber

SHEPHERD'S PIE

•DAIRY-FREE OPTION   •NUT-FREE   •EGG-FREE   •GRAIN-FREE
•GLUTEN-FREE

This shepherd's pie is low-carb, thanks to the mashed cauliflower instead of the usual mashed potatoes, but you can certainly use mashed potatoes or other mashed root instead of the cauliflower if you prefer. The filling for the pie is actually my Sloppy Joes recipe (page 145), but other fillings will work, too, such as leftover condensed soups, stews, and diced roasted meat and gravy. Or, if you're a vegetarian, lentil soup or stew works well with the cauliflower topping. I usually use an 8-inch (20-cm) round pie dish for this recipe, but a square one works as well.

2 ¼ pounds (1 kg) cauliflower (1 medium head), trimmed and cut into chunks

2 tablespoons (28 g) unsalted butter, ghee, or coconut oil

½ teaspoon salt, plus more to taste

1 to 2 tablespoons (15 to 30 ml) coconut milk or other kind of milk, or water, or as needed to cream the cauliflower

1 recipe Sloppy Joe (page 145)

1. Steam or boil the cauliflower until it is tender and a fork easily glides into it.

2. Preheat your oven to 400°F (200°C, or gas mark 6).

3. Cool the cauliflower for a few minutes and then place it in a food processor or high-speed blender. Add the butter, salt, and 1 tablespoon (15 ml) of the milk, and blend until it is creamy. Add more milk in small increments, only as needed to fully cream the cauliflower. Season to taste with salt and pepper.

4. Place the sloppy Joe mixture in a baking pan or pie dish and spread the creamed cauliflower evenly across the top. Sprinkle the top with salt and pepper and bake for 15 minutes, or until the pie is bubbling.

5. Serve warm. Store, covered, in the refrigerator for a few days.

YIELD: One 8-inch (20-cm) pie, or 4 servings

PER SERVING: 104 calories; 11 g carbohydrate; 6 g fat; 4 g protein; 5 g fiber

CHOOSE YOUR FILLING

For the meat filling, I've used everything from shredded roasted chicken to cut-up sausage. I've also made this meat-free by adding roasted vegetables

MEXICAN LASAGNA

•NUT-FREE   •GRAIN-FREE   •GLUTEN-FREE

Traditionally, lasagna is made with wide pasta noodles; however, coconut flour crêpes or tortillas are used here in their place. The Tortillas recipe (page 37) is already seasoned well for this dish, but if you prefer to use the Savory Crêpe recipe (page 73), just season it with ⅛ teaspoon salt and ¼ teaspoon cumin and a squeeze of lime juice (about 1 teaspoon [5 ml]).

5 ounces (142 g) spinach

1 cup (40 g) loosely packed cilantro

4 scallions

1 tablespoon (15 ml) coconut oil or other cooking oil

½ pound (225 g) ground chicken, turkey, or beef

¼ teaspoon chili powder

¼ teaspoon cumin

¼ teaspoon salt

1 can (14.5 ounce [411 g]) fire-roasted diced tomatoes with green chilies

6 to 8 Tortillas (page 37) or Savory Crêpes (page 73)

2 cups (200 g) shredded or grated Monterey Jack cheese or pepper Jack cheese, divided

⅛ teaspoon hot sauce or cayenne pepper (optional)

1. Preheat your oven to 425°F (220°C, or gas mark 7).

2. Finely chop the spinach, cilantro, and scallions.

3. Place a large saucepan over a medium heat. Add the oil and the ground chicken. Break up the chicken with a spatula as it cooks. Cook the chicken for a few minutes, or until it's almost done. Remove from saucepan and set aside.

4. Add the chopped spinach, cilantro, and scallions to the saucepan, then add the chili powder, cumin, salt, and fire-roasted tomatoes with chilies. Cook over medium heat for 5 minutes, stirring occasionally, and then turn off the heat.

5. In all the lasagna will have three layers. To make the first layer, place about two tortillas in an 8 × 8 × 2-inch (20 × 20 × 5-cm) baking dish, so they cover the bottom of the dish (you can cut to fit). Spoon one-third of the chicken mixture on top of the tortillas and then sprinkle on one-third of the shredded cheese. Cover with a second layer of tortillas and repeat with another one-third chicken mixture and one-third cheese. Add the last two tortillas, then the remaining chicken mixture, and finally the rest of the cheese.

6. Bake for 10 minutes, or until it is bubbling and the cheese is browning.

7. Cool for a few minutes and slice. Serve warm.

YIELD: 8 servings

PER SERVING: 160 calories; 3 g carbohydrate; 11 g fat; 11 g protein; 2 g fiber